HOW TO SURVIVE YOUR MONEY PROBLEMS

BANK
MUGGING POINT
CASH POINT

HOW TO SURVIVE YOUR MONEY PROBLEMS

Katharine Whitehorn

with drawings by Bill Tidy

Methuen

By the same author

WHITEHORN'S SOCIAL SURVIVAL
HOW TO SURVIVE IN HOSPITAL
HOW TO SURVIVE CHILDREN
HOW TO SURVIVE IN THE KITCHEN
ROUNDABOUT
ONLY ON SUNDAYS
OBSERVATIONS
SUNDAY BEST
VIEW FROM A COLUMN

(With Penguin Books)

COOKING IN A BEDSITTER

First published in 1983
by Methuen London Ltd
11 New Fetter Lane, London EC4P 4EE

Cover design by Bill Tidy

Phototypeset by Wyvern Typesetting Ltd, Bristol
Printed and bound in Great Britain by
Redwood Burn Ltd, Trowbridge

British Library Cataloguing in Publication Data

Whitehorn, Katharine
How to survive your money problems.
1. Finance, Personal
I. Title
332.024 HG179

ISBN 0-413-51560-5

CONTENTS

Before we begin:

First, this isn't a book for business men – and the self-employed will need something a good deal more comprehensive: it's just for the ordinary wage-slave trying to get by till payday.

Second, I've tried to keep figures down to a minimum because they change so fast; but where I have put them in, take it that they are 1983 figures and may change after that.

And finally, I ought in fairness to say that the countless knowledgeable people who have helped me are not responsible for any mistakes I've made – those, I assure you, are all my own work.

INTRODUCTION – WHO IS GOOD WITH MONEY?

Who is good with money? The sobersides who saves for a pension all his life? The property ace who borrows a hundred pounds and turns it into half a million? Or the girl who alternates frenzied bouts of selling off the furniture with equally frenzied trips to the Mediterranean but never worries about money at all?

The question isn't frivolous. There's no way we can get away from money: it runs through all our hands, even if in distressingly small amounts. But whether we're any good with it depends on what we think is the right way to live: you can't be good with money without deciding what you want the stuff for.

I know people that I think are good with money. An ICI director, for instance. When he started out as a print works foreman his boss was an explosive type who was always sacking people; our man saved £80 from his meagre pay against the day when he, too, would be out on his ear. He's sure the warm confidence that £80 gave him was the reason he never *was* sacked. By the time he got married, he was doing well enough to spend every penny of a £25 tax rebate on good claret for laying down.

Here's another. Even in the thirties, when he was alternately out of work, a balloon pilot, out of work, a cinema manager, out of work and then a journalist, a friend of mine had a great taste for expensive shoes and hand-made shirts. This made certain that, even when he had become well-known and well-paid, he almost always had a healthy overdraft. Then one day he heard of a chance to buy a freehold within yards of Piccadilly; and luckily had a bank manager who said, 'This opportunity we cannot afford to miss'. They set up a mortgage, and put in a tenant whose rent took care of the repayments. Of course if he'd lived sensibly he wouldn't always have had a whopping overdraft – but he wouldn't have ended up with this marvellous apartment either.

A ship-owner's son I know doesn't approve of inherited wealth, so he simply gave away three-quarters of his – I'd call that good with money: he knew what he wanted. Far better, anyway, than another heir I heard of who was so stunned by his inheritance that he's become quite mean.

He sees himself as the unworthy guardian of his grandfather's industry, and his wife isn't allowed so much as to take a taxi, let alone have a car of her own.

'I say, Mum, I've got £70 and an idea – if you'll keep us for three months we can get out this magazine.' That was the student founder of *Time Out* talking, and he never went back to college at all. He and his mates did fine with the magazine – and it was partly because, in the early years, they *all* lived on the same pittance, whether they were selling space, writing huge articles or brewing up the tea. He knew what it was about, all right.

The final cautionary tale concerns a family in *The Money Game* by Adam Smith (not *the* Adam Smith). A man got in on the ground floor with IBM shares, and watched them increase in value. Before he died he told his son, 'Don't whatever you do sell the IBM', so his son worked hard and got a mortgage; ultimately he left the shares to his son, pointing out that anyone who'd ever sold IBM had regretted it, so *he* worked hard, got a mortgage . . . three generations living exactly as if they had never had that money at all. I don't call them good with money – what's money *for*, anyway?

All this may not seem relevant to you and me, just trying to get by till the end of the month. But it is. However little room you have to manœuvre, until you know what you want from money, you can't decide what is a bad plan and what is a good one.

An accountant can tell you how to save for a safe old age – but if it means you never go abroad, never break out and buy a sports car or a bejewelled bracelet, then it's a good policy only if security's all you care about. Conversely, he could say, 'Look, put your money in Consolidated Goldmines and you'll double it' – and so you may; but if you're the type to stay awake at night worrying about it, then it simply isn't worth it for you.

Feelings are as important as facts, and half the money troubles people have come from not being able to tell them apart. A husband thinks they 'can't afford' his wife's new dress – that doesn't mean there's no money to buy it, but that Extravagance will tempt an evil providence; she thinks she needs it, to boost her flagging morale; the row isn't actually about money at all. The same with the teenager's jacket – is black leather 'worth' sixty quid? Not to his father, no – but to him it's a badge of manhood. A woman may reckon that the price of an evening's beers would be far better spent on food – but to the man who buys them, the money's paying for knowing he's still a man among his mates and not just a downtrodden breadwinner; what he's buying is not to be calculated simply in pounds and pints.

One of the silliest things the government ever wasted money on was an attempt to site a Third London Airport by 'costing' such things as trees, and church spires, and the misery of sitting fifty minutes in a bus. It simply cannot be done. Better to admit the limitations of financial facts, and give to feelings their due. Money is not a rigid absolute with hard and fast objective laws; it's as mystical, fluid and irrational as sex or religion – though anyone who uses it as a substitute for either is a mug.

So: having admitted all that, how to cope with money? Here are a few questions to ask.

What do I really want from the money?

Is the life you're leading the one you want – or just the one you're stuck with? Do you want to change it? You don't want to keep saying 'some day' and then find it's all too late – it is *very difficult* to get up the Pyramids with a pacemaker and a wooden leg.

What am I really paying for?

Whether it's a set of cushions or a headland in the Bahamas it's a vital question. You may think because you're paying more money, that you're getting better quality, when actually you're paying for soft lights and more polite salesgirls – which might be worth it, if you make better judgements in such circumstances. Ask: is the car expensive because it goes well – or because it's red and overstyled and makes me feel like a racing driver? Does the school give a better education, or am I really only paying for an OK accent? Am I getting a sounder house for more money – or buying my way into a better neighbourhood? The thing is to know what you're doing.

Have I got the evidence?

It may seem trivial, but my hat, it's not. Whether you're trying to get the money back on a faulty toaster, claiming the cleaning of your diamonds off the income tax or persuading social security you need extra money for heating, the bills, the receipts, the cheque book stubs, the copies of the letters are essential. I've often thought paper was actually our religion – no transaction valid till the sacred stuff's changed hands; it's certainly crucial where money's concerned.

Am I keeping up with the times?

If you worked in the thirties, you may think that playing safe is the only way to manage money. If you grew up in the sixties, you may be quite unused to taking thought for the morrow – until you wind up in the bankruptcy court. What was a good job opportunity in the seventies may be a dead end in the eighties; a good investment last year may be a terrible one next year. Pull your attitudes out occasionally and give them a shake – it may be time for a change.

Do I understand it?

Whatever you're thinking of doing with your money, if you don't understand it, don't do it – whatever your brother-in-law's wheeler-dealer friend recommends. Apart from anything else, if you don't understand it, you won't know when it might need changing.

DO YOU NEED . . . ?

An accountant?

Yes – but not necessarily all the time. People who are self-employed and/or have tricky tax problems need an accountant on a chronic basis, so to speak; but most people could do with the equivalent of the occasional check-up: just to see that their mortgage/loan/savings/tax code and so on are in order. £30 for a one-off accountant's appointment is probably well worthwhile, especially if your circumstances are changing – e.g. before retirement. Get the right one, though – ask around among people in your own trade. We suffered for years under a righteous Scotsman who was marvellous with City firms but had scarcely heard of actual people; it's horses for courses where you can.

A bank?

Almost certainly, yes. Your bank manager may make you feel the way you did in your old headmaster's study, but he's useful in several ways. A bank is usually the best place to go for a loan. There are useful things it can do e.g. advise with tax, spread your payments with a budget account (see p. 19). Probably not a good idea, whatever they say, to have a bank as an executor. They are amazingly slow and cannot, obviously, bend a single rigid regulation to help a widow along, as might a couple of old friends and a nephew.

A bank is a place where they lend you an umbrella in fair weather and ask for it back when it begins to rain.

Robert Frost

A Solicitor?

For house conveyancing, yes, there are too many pitfalls. For wills, certainly – and it's the best bargain they do: only £15, sometimes. The point is that even simple wills can get complex by accident if you've worded it wrong: for example, here was this chap leaving half his money to his son and the rest to the son's 'dear wife Felicity'; the kind old Catholic hadn't considered the possibility that it might be the dear wife Fiona by then. A good solicitor can also advise how, for example, to pass on some of the property ahead of time to avoid Capital Transfer Tax. For divorce, possibly – but keep it to a minimum – see Splitting Up p. 62. You can often get half an hour for £5 just to assess the scale of your problem, whether it's going to be worth getting more involved and maybe running into far larger costs.

A Will?

Of course you do – if you die intestate (disgusting word) it will take ages to sort out who gets what, it probably won't be what you'd have chosen and the lawyers will get most of the money.

Credit cards?

Mainly a matter of temperament. I have a complete set of plastic cards, but my family think the question should rather be: Do I need my head examined? It does, of course, make some difference which bits of plastic you're talking about . . . read on.

If all the rich men in the world divided up their money amongst themselves there wouldn't be enough to go round.

Jules Bertillon

PLASTIC CARDS

People get muddled between the bits of plastic which seem to do beautifully instead of money. Allow me to deal you in on the plastic pack.

1 **Cheque Card** – this is the one with £50 on it, and blue: you use it with a cheque. Bank guarantees to pay up if signature matches the one on the card, so shopkeepers will accept your cheque.

2 **Instant money card** – called different things by different banks, Service-Card, Checkpoint etc. Outside large banks there is a magic machine: you put in your card, punch a secret number on its buttons and lo! it gives you money. Some banks let you go on getting money like this even if you're overdrawn; others will simply swallow your card with an evil gulp if there's no money in your account. Some banks are now combining this with the Cheque Card, or with Access.

3 **True Credit cards** – Access and Visa. These allow you to charge things you buy up to a credit limit, which is different for each person; if you pay at once there's no charge, but if you let it run they charge a per cent – which says something like 1.5% per month – deceptive – that works out at 19.5% per year – a lot. Jolly useful for spreading the agony, though. You can also use them to get cash across the counter from a bank. It pays *either* to pay off in full within the stated time *or* just the little bit they say you must. If you pay off half of it, the interest on what remains works out high. **Barclaycard** is both Visa and Barclays Bank cheque card in one – i.e. equivalent to the two cards of, say, a Nat West cheque card and an Access.

4 **So-called Credit cards** – American Express, Diners: you pay an annual subscription (plus a tiny amount to insure against someone stealing it, if you've any sense) and they send you the bill each month. No per cent charge until it's forty days overdue – you're supposed to pay at once. You can get cash at American Express offices.

MAFIA

5 **Limited credit cards** for certain shops or chains (e.g. of garages). Two kinds: one just like American Express etc. but only for the one shop – they know you will feel it's painless to shop with them, rather than somewhere you have to pay actual cash. The other relates to a credit arrangement; details vary but you are paying a set rate of interest. (Watch the APR – Annual Percentage Rate – see p. 22.)

There are also the **Gold Cards** which are supposed to prove that you are stinking rich, more honest than George Washington and a personal friend of Prince Charles; American Express Gold Card gives you, it says here, automatic credit with Lloyds up to £7,000. Lloyds, however, say there's nothing automatic about it and they take a long, hard look at you first.

Come for your inheritance – you may have to pay for the funeral.

Yiddish proverb

DEBT AND CREDIT

'At least I can say we've never been in debt', says Fred smugly; while his children watch wistfully as Bill, who has no such reservations, takes his kids around in a car on HP, pays for meals with a Barclaycard and has a video on a credit loan from the shop. Who is right?

It's certainly true that plenty of people recently have been living the normal life of the 80s (Bill's life) and suddenly found they were out of work and in trouble. But it's also true that the Freds of this world can miss out on a great deal they could perfectly well have had – and that can even go for their homes: mortgages are the last word in respectability these days, but the Victorians thought they were as dodgy as Hire Purchase.

Money Which? did a careful chart about whether it is slightly cheaper, on a given object, to buy it by credit and pay interest, or buy it with cash and lose the interest on the money because you've spent it. My guess is that if you're the sort of person who does that kind of sum with any frequency or any success, you aren't reading this book anyway; so I suggest that you look at it another way.

How are you going to *feel* about it? There's nothing immoral about credit, but it might, quite simply, be more fun to save up and then go out, gloating, to get the thing, rather than to have it now and incur just one more bloody bill to be paid at the end of the month. There again, it might not. If you've wanted a boat, say, since you were four, and you can now get it with a bit of boat finance, why do yourself out of those three years you could be floating around in it? And how, anyway, calculate the amount of money you might have paid on other holidays while waiting to have enough money saved for the boat?

God is love but get it in writing.

Gypsy Rose Lee

It's feelings and facts again. My father-in-law prides himself on never having been in debt; he lived frugally, educated his children well (before the war, when it was school fees or nothing), and ended up with his own house and a car and pretty much the life-style he wanted. So did my father – who only ever grasped one fact about finance, which is that the value of money goes down; at the beginning of the war his salary was £500 and our school fees were £450. The size of his overdraft never bothered him; he wasn't frightened of bank managers – he knew they made their money by lending, however much they might talk (and look) like constipated clergymen denouncing Sin. As far as I can see the outcome of both financial policies was exactly the same; it was just a question of how the two men felt about it.

WHERE DID IT ALL GO?

'They can't understand it,' the bank manager said jovially. 'They don't drink, they don't go out, they all lead very frugal lives. Then you say, "What's that?" "Oh, that's a weekend away with friends, that was only £200."'

Agonisingly biting our Biros back to the clip, we go over it all: it *can't* be that much overdrawn – can it? The sordid answer is yes it can: and it might help, next time, to work out what happened. One thing you can/should do is to write down a budget of all the unamusing things you can't get out of – gas, electricity, rates, rent, fares and so forth. That total will immediately depress you to such an extent that you reach for a large Scotch – so the next thing you'd better write down is 'Scotch'. I'm told that when they do polls about how much people say they drink, and how much drink is nationally consumed, the figures nowhere near match; nobody allows themselves to realise how much they actually put away.

More tenuous are the black holes into which one's money is sucked because, for some reason, they *don't count*. Christmas is the worst, of course; but cries like 'It's her birthday!' or 'After all we are on holiday' cost a lot of money. Illness doesn't count – all the way from taking a taxi home because you're too ill for the bus queue to getting flowers, getting convenience food, getting a new book because someone close to you is in hospital. Nor does the vet count (but see insurance); emergencies don't count, or funerals, or the TV licence, which never gets allowed for. I suspect the key to this is that we've all got morals and money so mixed up that we feel if we can't be *blamed* for spending the money, then it won't figure on the debit side of the bank account – but it does.

Money is like a sixth sense; without it you cannot make a complete use of the other five.

Somerset Maugham

ARE YOU A SPENDER?

If you're one of the world's great spenders, there are ways of outwitting yourself.

You can operate **the five week month**. Some months are nearly five weeks anyway; but if you always divide your monthly paycheck into five units for thinking purposes, not four, you're more likely to have a pleasant surprise than the usual grisly shock at the end of the month.

Topping up the cheques is another device – you have to pay a cheque for £6.60, for example. What you write on the counterfoil is £7.00 – again, pleasant surprises may accrue. Only snag is, if you're trying to trace a cheque through the computer and all they've recorded is the amount, you won't immediately be able to identify which cheque was which.

Spreading the load. Organised people put by so much for gas, so much for electricity, so much for TV whereas you and me. . . . It helps us, therefore, to spend our way into solvency by buying those stamps you can get for gas, electricity and TV at the post office. You stick them on a card, and there they are when the bills come in. Rates, gas and electricity can all be paid by arrangement where the cost is spread evenly over the months, to save a huge terrifying bill every quarter or half year.

Another way is to have one of those spreading accounts – called different names at different banks – where you estimate the hideous bills for the year, and have a proportion of your salary paid into a

---

Inflation in the sixties was just a nuisance to be endured, like varicose veins or French foreign policy.

Bernard Levin

---

separate account for these things; then you can, with a separate cheque book, pay those bills as they come in without fear – the bank has arranged to spread it all out evenly.

Bone Burying – I don't know why I bother to recommend this since all dogs and most housewives do it anyway. But if you leave a few coins in any handbag or pocket when you change to a different one, you've something to scratch around for when the milkman arrives and you've no cash.
N.B. NEVER tell the children where you keep it.

Spenders are also the people who need **piggy banks**, the ones who should carelessly dribble 20p pieces into an old Dimpled Haig bottle; only trouble is, they're all too likely to buy the Haig first at ten quid a time.

A fool and his money are soon parted. What I want to know is how they got together in the first place.

Cyril Fletcher

IT'S YOUR MONEY THEY'RE AFTER

The world is full of smart-alecs, some of whom actually believe what they're saying – it's always more convincing if you deceive yourself before setting out to con the customer. Some are straight sharks. Either way, we live in a nasty world.

Sales techniques, as taught to the man on the move, include getting irritated or overbearing – they hope you'll buy something just to placate them; they include **the hard luck story**, so be sceptical of people who come round saying they're students or unemployed or will bring you good luck – treat gypsies like Jehovah's Witnesses and vice versa. In fact never buy anything **on the doorstep** unless (1) it's a known firm – Avon or Kleenezee (2) they leave you literature and are prepared to call back – **never sign** anything on a first call; or (3) you are just feeling soft-hearted and rich and don't mind being cheated.

Jungle areas include **second-hand cars** – there's no way for the odd outsider to tell what a car's like, and little tips like looking for clouds of blue smoke only give you a false feeling of security. Get the AA or RAC to check out any car you're planning to buy – and *don't* be hustled by some notion that someone else is after the car, so there's no time for a check – that's part of the game, too. **Garages** have been known to conceal a second Access form under the one you're signing, and so debit an extra sum; either riffle through to see they haven't, or check the Access account with some care.

Shop assistants often get more commission on some goods than others, so don't pay much attention to what they say (I once flattered a leading consumer lady into buying a one-sleeved dress that had an extra commission on it because it was regarded as unsaleable). Loud **fake auctions** have fake buyers in the audience bumping up the bidding, you won't get a bargain there. **Restaurants** can go on adding a service per cent to the VAT and the VAT to the figure that includes service almost indefinitely – watch it. And if a shop has a ludicrously cheap '**loss leader**' to lure you in (or a book or record club has a free introductory item) you should have no qualm whatever about buying just that, nothing else. They're trying to con you – but you're outsmarting them. It isn't immoral.

Be doubly careful about any tempting prospect that seems to be after your savings, your redundancy money or whatever. You think a course in mending holes in the road would be a good standby, you pay for it and learn how to apply hot sludge with the aid of a special machine – and then find yourself asking how many people you know who *want* holes in their roads mended, anyway. Someone tries to sell you a franchise to sell something – well, possibly. But read the fine print: if part of the deal is that you should then go and recruit other people (it's known as pyramid selling, and there are modified as well as out-and-out forms of it) don't touch it.

Don't be an APRil fool

'Only £6 a month!' trills the ad. 'Monthly interest rate 1.75%', says the credit card soothingly. Behind this may be concealed a whopping large rate of yearly interest – and nowadays anyone selling you anything on credit has to say what the **Annual Percentage Rate** (APR) actually is. If it's not mentioned, the people are crooks and you'd best not be dealing with them at all. The real snare to watch out for is the finance company which offers you a loan with no fixed time limit on it. Why? Because if you fall behind on interest by even a day – and you will – they'll add that to your total indebtedness: 'How is it,' asked one woman bleakly, 'that I borrowed £10,000 ten years ago, I've been paying £30 a month and I *still* owe £10,000?' That's how.

Getting it back

A shop doesn't have to refund your money if you've simply changed your mind – but if there's something wrong with the goods, don't be fobbed off with a credit note – stand there and make as noisy a fuss as you can.

I would like to quote what a judge said long ago: that all his experience both as Counsel and Judge had been spent sorting out the difficulties of people who, upon the recommendation of people they did not know, signed documents which they did not read, to buy goods they did not need, with money they had not got.

Gilbert Harding

---

bear to. Even sale goods must be 'of merchantable quality' so if there's positively a hole in your boot, take it back.

If you want to sue someone in a county court, you can, though it helps to consult a consumer agency first – a Citizens Advice Bureau is free or the *Which?* Personal Service costs £20 a year from 14 Buckingham Street, London WC2 (you have to pay this by Banker's Order). Otherwise, you can get an application form from the court office (address in telephone directory, under Courts); you give brief details and there's a small fee. Everyone says the process is informal and unfrightening, so if the problem is less than £5,000 and you're getting nowhere with the firm, go ahead. No lawyers needed. You can get a couple of pamphlets – *Small Claims in the County Court* and *Enforcing Money Judgements in the County Court* – free from the Lord Chancellor's Office or from Citizens Advice Bureaux.

All money nowadays seems to be produced with a natural homing instinct for the Treasury.

Prince Philip (Civil List £179,300)

VAT

'Vat is VAT?'
'You mean what is love?'
'NO. I know vat is luf. I vant to know vat is VAT?'
'No man ever knew what is what.'

Punch

Just so. You pay a restaurant bill that has 15% VAT on it. Each quarter your restaurateur forwards this sum to Customs and Excise. But he has been buying fish, paper napkins, bread, soap etc. in pursuit of his business; and he can claim back from the Customs and Excise all the VAT money that he has paid on these things. So can you claim back *your* VAT, too? No, not unless you're registered for VAT, which there's no point in being unless you are yourself a business. If you bring in more than £18,000 (this sum changes) in self-employed earnings (freelancing, say) you don't have a choice: you must register for VAT, and they send you piles of incomprehensible papers, and a kind man comes round to explain it all to you. Sometimes he can be heard screaming in the street afterwards.

Builders estimates are often given *without* VAT, so remember to add it on mentally or you'll get a nasty shock. You may anyway, of course, since an estimate (hopeful guess) is not the same as a quotation (offer to do the work for a given sum).

If you are truly serious about preparing your child for the future, don't teach him to subtract – teach him to deduct.

Fran Lobowitz

INCOME TAX

We all pay it – or almost all; we remind ourselves that the Dobermann Pinscher, terrible hound, was developed by a German tax-collector to help him in his work; we see other people apparently getting away with murder and setting the cost of the axe against the Capital Transfer Tax on the assets of the victim. And we don't understand any of it.

Actually ordinary income tax is about the simplest bit to understand, at least if you're straightforwardly employed. You are allowed so much (tax allowance) before they start to take any of it away – this year it's £1,785 for a single person, £2,795 for a married man; a wife working gets a wife's earning allowance which is the same as the single person's allowance, and if you're bringing up a child on your own there's an additional person allowance. If you've got dependents, or various special problems, you get allowances for them. After that, it's taxed at the basic rate until you get £14,000 when it goes up by stages. Your *code* which appears on your pay slip is the first three of the four figures of your allowance, plus the letter denoting your status.

L is single person or wife's earnings allowance; H married man's or additional person (see p. 63); P is age allowance for one, V age allowance for a couple. D followed by a number means one of the higher rates of tax. E means Emergency – or that they are digging into you for something not paid earlier on, and T is splendid – it's what they give you when you've told the taxman you don't want your firm to know *what* your code is – presumably because you're chatting up the girls in Accounts and you don't want them to know you're married.

If you think you've been given the wrong code, you can go round to a tax office and ask; and apparently three million people do this a year so they're used to it.

What about deductions? There's not much for employed people: you might get clothes maintenance from £336 for an army officer to a few pounds for washing your overalls (ask your trade union if there's an agreed rate). You might get the cost of, say, your chisels if you're a carpenter or your camera if you're the office photographer, but dreams of being a freelance and deducting everything, from your house to your helicopter to your mistress (oh you ineluctable deductable you) are vain. The self-employed have to take off all this – light, heat, car and so on – just as a firm has to take away the cost of lighting the factory and the vans and buying the plastic before it can say it's made a profit.

Capital Gains Tax is an attempt to tax people who make their money buying and selling things, e.g. stocks and shares, houses etc. and **Capital Transfer Tax** is like the old death duties except it applies to gifts while you're living as well. You can give away any amount of money so long as you live for ten years afterwards. Whatever you give away in the ten years prior to your death will be exempt from Capital Transfer Tax if it's less than £55,000; the balance of your assets will be taxed on a sliding scale. Above that figure it gets somewhat complicated and you'd best get a solicitor or an accountant to sort it out.

See also p. 34 tax and married couples, p. 78 tax in retirement, p. 42 maternity.

IN TRANSITION

All people are equal, we're told, but not between sixteen and twenty-five they're not. What happens to you financially during this transition from school to the outer world can vary wildly according to what category the powers that be have deemed you belong in.

If you're over sixteen and simply still at school, a sixth form college, a tertiary, FE or technical college, you are, on the whole, reckoned to be your parents' headache. If they're very hard up, you may get an Educational Maintenance Award, but they're not large, not easy to come by and fast diminishing. If you're unemployed and trying to add a qualification or two while you hope for work, you come under a bundle of restrictions designed to make sure that you would take the work if it was offered to you. You have to be on Supplementary Benefit (if you're still living at home you get the non-householder's rate, which is a bit less than what you're expected to live on by yourself). At the moment the regulations for this say you can study for up to twenty-one hours, but you must have been waiting hopefully for a job for three months before you can qualify – and as you can't sign on until the September after you quit school, you can't qualify till December/January. They do, however, let you go on a course for fifteen hours a week while you're waiting for a course – but then you have to *change* courses after the three months. Sounds crazy – and who am I to say it isn't?

If you are safely into a college of higher or further education or on teacher training or any other course 'designated' by the Department of Education, you get a mandatory grant, the local authority pays your fees and if your parents have any money they're expected to help pay for you – you just get the minimum basic grant. In this context, you're not regarded as independent till you're twenty-five. There are a few odd courses, occupational therapy for instance, which somehow aren't designated, for which all the same you might get a 'discretionary' grant instead.

The Youth Training Scheme gives people £25 a week for a year while they train, and fights are already breaking out in lecture-rooms between those who somehow still count as school kids and get nothing and those who are in the scheme. It's still in its chaotic early stages: ask a careers officer or at the Job Centre, or the British Youth Council, 57 Chalton Street, London NW1 (tel. 01–387 7559).

To know more about all this, either get in touch with the National Union of Students grants officer at 461 Holloway Rd. London N7 (tel. 01–272 8900) or see a book called *Second Chance* by Andrew Pates and Martin Good, £4.95 from Great Ouse Press, 82 Castle St, Cambridge CB3 0AJ. It's helpful even if it's your first chance, as they actually seem to understand the ins and outs of the system. So do Youth Aid, who are at 9 Poland Street, London W1 (tel. 01–439 8523/4).

Living on the meagre sums you may get given is another matter; there is a limit to the number of Spudulikes you can eat. Some students eke out the grant by living with a family and babysitting instead of paying rent; and it is not unknown for Student A in Edinburgh to swap families with Student B in Glasgow so that no money changes hands but both get a chance to live away from home.

Even if you're only a student for a few months, it's probably worth it just for the student card (get it from the NUS or your student union), which is a passport to a lot of reduced rates here and abroad for things like trains, buses, art galleries. The Young Person's Rail Card, however, where you pay £12 for the card and then go half fare almost anywhere (with some restrictions), is available to anyone under twenty-four whether they're studying or not (and mature students). Students may also think that now is the time to get a bank account – the banks are so certain that the students of today are the high earners of tomorrow that they'll offer you free banking for at least a year, and as grants aren't keeping pace with inflation you may well need an overdraft. In the unlikely event of your being able to earn money in the holidays, you'll be cheered to hear that you don't have to pay tax on it – provided it's not over the allowed amount. NUS also runs a discount scheme for a lot of consumer durables and they have cut-rate insurance schemes too.

FLAT-SHARING

Sharing a flat is the obvious method of getting away from your parents without having to go on the streets (in either sense); keeps the costs down, and it's friendly. But someone has to be one to whom the place is actually assigned, on the agreement or the lease; and it's that one who is legally responsible if all the others decamp without paying. If you're the one that's carrying the can it is *not* being mean to ask for a month's or a week's rent in advance (however you pay your rent) – how are you suddenly to get a new flatmate, or pay double the rent?

Ways of making it a fair deal include:

Have the rent-book in one name, the electricity bill in the name of one of the others, the gas bill sent to a third; then you've an equal stake.

Make those who are paying their rent also provide some of the stamps you can get for electricity and gas.

Put in a payphone – it's more expensive, of course, but less ruinous than having one of you leave for Venezuela without paying for all those calls he's been making to fix things up over there. Or – cheaper – get a meter fitted on the phone to monitor how much a call costs.

Make everyone put money into a common purse at the beginning of a student term (or when they get paid) and pay all bills out of that. Some sharers alternate the cooking, so that one person copes each week, putting the food money, only, into a common purse – though it's a bit apt to contain nothing but IOU slips when you desperately need cash for eggs for the weekend.

Drink is a problem mainly if you have a teetotaller in your midst who doesn't contribute because she doesn't drink, but her guests do – they drink yours. Otherwise each buys in turn or you have separate stores.

There was a time when a fool and his money were soon parted; now it happens to everyone.

Adlai Stevenson

COUPLES AND COSTS

Dividing up the money isn't necessarily any more complex when you're a couple – married or that sort of thing – than when you're sharing a flat; you should see some flatmates carving every sausage into three pieces. But it's infinitely more fraught with emotion.

Doubtless some very rich couples come together without making any coherent arrangement, she paying the insurance on her diamonds and the staff in the house in Mustique, he coughing up for the penthouse in Belgravia. For the rest of us, there always has to be some plan, however chaotic. You might consider which of the following broad intentions suits you best.

One pot – e.g. a joint account or a common purse. Both put into it everything they get; both can draw on it. Advantages are that 'it isn't my money, it's *our* money'; both get an equal crack at it, and both should know equally how it's draining away. It takes care of fluctuating earnings, and if she earns more than he does and he minds, it fudges the issue nicely. It helps to have a rule that all payments over, say, £100 get discussed first.

But the drawbacks are great. It's even harder to know exactly how you stand – maybe *he* drew out that last £50 this morning. An extravagant partner can never say, 'I'll skinflint on six things and splurge on the seventh' – there's a sort of moral obligation to keep the spending low on everything, which may make it a lot easier to waste money on ten cheap things than spend it sensibly on one big one. It's a mess if you split up, and I've known one husband keep an extra account his wife didn't know about, so that she saved and scrimped on their (visibly empty) joint account, while he hid huge amounts elsewhere.

Even if you have a joint pot, there is a case for *agreeing* allowances – so much for food, so much for clothes, so much for holidays etc.

Two pots His money, her money. If both are earning, they agree who pays for what – one copes with the rates, gas etc., the other with food, for example; if only one is earning, he 'gives' the non-earning one an allowance for housekeeping and (let us hope) some personal spending money. Advantage is that each feels in control of their money, which is psychologically important; if they're very together there's not necessarily any problem about one of them paying a bill the other usually takes care of, if he/she is skint. Drawbacks can be endless wrangling about who pays for what – she always paid for the food, for example, when she was working full-time; now she's home with two kids and a piffling part-time job but somehow she's still stuck with it; or he gets all the dreary bills like insurance, mortgage, rates and she gets all the fun ones like clothes and holidays. Couples with two accounts and one car are forever running out of petrol trying not to be the one who has to fill the tank.

If this is the system you operate, it's important to review the thing from time to time, to see whether rising prices and rising and falling paychecks still match as they did at the beginning. An annual review, however agonising, can clear a lot of air.

Three pots His, hers and ours. For couples where both are earning this is a good one – just as it works excellently for, say, three people sharing a flat or a holiday. Each pays an agreed sum into a common kitty for joint things, but keeps control of a personal sum. Its advantage is that you can adjust, if you like, on the 'from each according to his ability' principle, yet anyone can pay the bills as they come up. You do get arguments about whether his golf club subscription ('but you do come for drinks there sometimes') or the Moulinex ('you eat it, after all') should or should not come out of the common pot; and of course it doesn't work at all if someone rats on the deal and doesn't pay in. Trouble comes when a wife stops work to raise babies and the husband is entirely unbraced to pay a sum *into* her own account – he may need to be made to realise that this is not actually unfair.

You might think that such a comparatively simple matter as payment for shared expenses could be easily dealt with by one of these systems; you might, that is, if you'd never actually met any human beings. But saying that is like saying that in sex, you place A into B, what's the problem? It is all much more complex and emotional than that, because money means such different things to different people.

Academics, cheerfully pooling their salaries with their mates and unable to see why everyone else doesn't do the same, don't realise they get their status from being Ph.D. or the coming man in liver flukes; they don't understand that to a business man, to whom money is how you keep score, an inability to buy a round of doubles because there's nothing in the joint account can affect not just his temper but his whole feelings about his own manliness. He may well be the one who subtly downgrades his wife's earnings in importance – it's an insidious process by which you say 'by the time we've paid for her to have some decent clothes and a bicycle and a babysitter it's scarcely worth her working at all' – a process of reasoning he would certainly not apply to his own salary, first discounting the car, his suits, the tax.

Conversely, a wife who has felt put down because she was the one who had to *ask* for money all the time can come to value the stuff as a symbol of personal independence: not liable, as his always has been, to be used on dreary things like the gas bill and the mortgage repayments. Then she can cause immense resentment by flashing about being 'generous' to the kids with treats and new clothes, while Daddy just goes on boringly paying for the roof over their heads.

There is no easy answer to any of this. But one or two things certainly make it worse. First is the habit, quite prevalent even today, of a man not telling his wife how much he earns. This may once have been all right – up to a point – when a husband could protect his wife from ever bothering her pretty little head about such things – though at the levels where money was really tight, often enough it was the woman who ran the whole show, taking over the pay packet and giving a man just enough back for his beer and tobacco.

But nowadays it simply isn't on. If he doesn't come clean about what he earns, why should she, when it's her turn (and statistically she's more than likely to be back at work eventually)? Husbands complain, traditionally, of the extravagance of wives – but if a wife doesn't know how much her husband earns, the word has no meaning – extravagant meaning 'more than is reasonable'. She can't *know* what's reasonable. Ah, but I'll tell her, the husband might say. Possibly. But just let me tell you about my great-aunt, who scrimped and saved her entire life, cutting a potato in half so there would be a piece for each of them and keeping careful score of the umpteen relations who had slept in the spare bed before she finally broke out and changed the sheets. When the great-uncle died, he cut up for £22,000 – an enormous sum at the time. So at last she bought the classical music LPs she'd longed for – about ten months before she grew too deaf to hear them.

Anyone thinking of getting married to someone who is mean or secretive about money ought to wonder, quite seriously, whether this is just family habit, or a temporary hang-up, or a really bad omen for the future. It's the experiences of those who *were* married that make such depressing reading – women, for example, who had been married to quite well-off men who say they are now better off separated and on Social Security (which is, in spite of that chap with £200 a week the *Daily Mail* keeps interviewing, the equivalent of being *dirt* poor); or men who turned their pay-packet over to their wives and weren't even allowed beer money back.

The worst abuses simply couldn't happen if everyone was honest about what they earned, and what everything cost, from the start; that way, at least you'd know what you were fighting about.

Fight? Actually, yes. Few things are more destroying to the feel of a home than a constant, obsessive, niggle-niggle-niggle about should she have bought those cigarettes, should he have taken a taxi; far better to have one or two really roof-raising rows and get it sorted out.

Let me quote from Basil Boothroyd's *Let's Stay Married* on the subject – the wife speaking: '"He'd lock himself away for an evening, with the bills and his cheque-book and the whisky, and come down about ten o'clock looking white and overdrawn . . . on the whole I remained detached from the seamy side."' Then she kept having bills sent back because he'd paid an old receipt, or put the decimal point in the wrong place: '"It turned out that he always did the accounts with his eyes half closed to filter the pangs of parting. . . . So we had a stormy scene that only true love could weather, and now I write the cheques and take the blame."

'"Blame for what?"

'"For what they come to, what else? When he's not writing the cheques he gets the idea there aren't any to write."'

This is half the trouble; that neither of you really understands the other's area of spending. So one piece of therapy that can work wonders is to swap for a bit: let *him* see if he can feed three kids on that amount; let *her* try writing the cheques for the insurance, the rates, the gas bill. . . . It has to be for long enough, of course, for the full horror of it all to sink in; no good letting him just eat all the tins in the cupboard or her dodge the quarterly electricity bill.

If that's impossible, try keeping accounts for a couple of months – though it's not foolproof, I admit. We did it once, and my husband carefully scored petrol £10, beer £1.40, Cauliflower 20p, but then simply concluded 'eaten by mice: £10'.

Whatever system you finally work out, ask these questions about it. Are both of you able to spend, or forced to skimp, about equally? Does it give each of you *some* money to spend without having to account for it – even if it's only a tiny amount? Is it really fair shares, or is one party expected to be 'grateful' for their half of the family income? Have you worked out what will happen if circumstances change – if someone loses a job or has a baby or falls sick? And above all – do you both understand it?

TAX FOR TWO

When you get married, the wife stops getting a **single person's allowance** (owing to not being single) but the husband gets a **married man's allowance**, and if she earns, she gets a **wife's earned income allowance**, which is the same as the single person's allowance – but only on earnings, not all those dividends and such. (Tax allowances are what you're allowed to earn before the Inland Revenue starts taking anything.)

There are three ways of getting taxed. The **standard** way is for hubby to fill out the tax form, getting all info from devoted wife, and she never need know *his* income at all.

Or you can go for **wife's earnings election** (get form 14 from the tax office) which means that you each get the single person's allowance and the wife pays her own tax on her own earnings (though not, for some reason, on investment income – don't ask me why). Which you choose depends on how much you earn – high earners should go for wife's earnings election.

There's now a third thing, called **Separate Assessment** – this doesn't pay any better, it's just a different way of dividing things. By applying (on Form 11S which both husband and wife must sign) you each tell the taxman what you earn; he works out your total tax bill and splits it proportionately. Neither of you need know what the other earns at all, though I suppose if you were wildly mathematical you might be able to

---

I'm tired of love, I'm still more tired of rhyme
But money gives me pleasure all the time.

Hilaire Belloc

---

work it out. Total bill is the same as for the standard way, unless (are you with me?) you choose to have *both* wife's election *and* separate assessment, in which case it's the same total bill as for wife's earnings election.

When should you get married?

For the year you're married in, the wife goes on being taxed as a single person – but the man gets the married man's allowance all the same. So the sooner after April 6 (start of the tax year) the better.

Should you, in fact **get married at all**? Depends how much you earn. If you're normally not getting into high rates of tax, you'll do better wedded than just bedded, because of the married man's allowance. But once you get to the level where your earnings are being added together to bring you up into a high tax bracket – £22,600, say, but this varies from year to year – you might do better just to cohabit. You get double the tax relief on a hefty mortgage – ceiling is £30,000 for one at the moment, so you could go up to £60,000 for two. (Mortgage companies, I should say, and social security and so on nowadays don't usually care whether you're married or not.) But do people *really* decide these things on financial grounds?

Money can't buy friends, but it can get you a better class of enemy.

Spike Milligan

MORTGAGE

You have looked at four hundred homes, loathed most of them, dreamed about twenty and finally settled on one. Unless Daddy simply writes a cheque or you are waiting in agony to sell another house, the chances are you want to borrow the money. You can nowadays do this: (1) from the local authority – if you're lucky (2) from a building society (3) on a complicated form of insurance which may or may not be done through the building society and (4) – much to the building societies' annoyance – a bank.

A building society will usually reckon to lend you up to two and a half times the 'primary' salary (the bigger one, usually the man's) plus one times the secondary (as a rule of thumb, although considerable discretion upwards is exercised). But they don't always reckon it up as you might – they'll take off any commitments you already have (first wife, dependent relative etc.) before they start counting. So if you're paying an aged granny £50 a month you'd better keep quiet about her. In any case, don't assume they think you as credit-worthy as you do. They'll lend a proportion of the valuation of the house (which isn't the same as what you're paying for it – some of these new housing estate prices go up and down like yo-yos) and nowadays they'll let you see their valuation of what they think the shack is worth. 100% mortgages aren't too common, but you might get one on a house that doesn't cost more than a certain figure – it's £35,000 at the moment. Or you can occasionally borrow the deposit money from a bank.

One snag to reckon with is the time-lag. Each branch of a building society has so much per month to lend and you join a queue waiting for the money; maybe several months long. Abbey National will tell you ahead of time whether you *will* get the money, so you can go ahead, maybe asking a bridging loan from the bank – but the bank may well ask why you aren't borrowing it all from them anyway – and indeed you might: check the rates of interest. Building societies, by the way, do definitely favour people who've been saving with them – so before you start to save, check that the society is geared to give you what you want.

How long do you want to tie yourself up for? The answer, oddly, is as long as possible. Simply because the value of money does go down (even if this is slowing up a bit) the later you pay it all back the better off you are. And indeed, when it's all over, if you're with the Abbey National you can keep 50p in your mortgage account, and it isn't as loony as it sounds: the deeds are safe with the Society, you don't have to pay a bank to store them; and if you want to borrow more – to put on a sun-room, say, or a dungeon for the grandchildren – it's all set up; you don't have to pay legal fees again, and it's still called a mortgage with attendant tax relief.

There are basically four types of mortgage, and you had better sit down with a damp cloth on your head and get someone – *not* the smart-alec insurance salesman – to explain it all in detail.

There's a straight **repayment** mortgage – OK, but the repayment rates go up and down (as with all Building Society mortgages) and, to protect the house if the main breadwinner dies, you have to take out a separate Mortgage Protection Policy. There is a **with-profits endowment mortgage** – this is expensive, but when you do pay it off, you get a lump sum at the end; if you die, the house is your widow's outright. (I say 'widow' but you can set it up so that if either earner dies, it works the same.) A **non-profit endowment mortgage** is much the same, but with no lump sum – *Money Which?* says it's the Worst Buy. And there's a **lower-cost endowment mortgage**: not so pricey as a with-profits, nor so negligible as the non-profit; probably if you can afford it your best bet.

You do get tax relief on the interest part of all this; and the means by which they do it is changing. The scheme called MIRAS (Mortgage Interest Relief At Source) means that instead of you paying, and then claiming back the relief in your tax coding (see p. 26), you pay an amount that's already taken account of your tax relief, and then the mortgage company claims it back from the Government. It's more their headache than yours, mercifully, but it means that what happened when your friend got a house five years ago won't be the same as what's to happen now.

Everything about moving house – solicitor, conveyancing, removal, new curtains, change of address cards – is *always* going to cost more than you expected. So when you look at a house, it's worth asking yourself how much of what needs doing to it must be done at once (e.g. mend the roof, fix the broken lock) and how much – making French windows, classy tile floor – could wait. Perhaps this is also the place to mention that you need insurance from the *moment* the place is yours: thieves rush in where builders fear to tread, and pretty silly you look when they've taken all the copper piping.

Whether you want a house at all is an interesting point. To some of us – most, maybe – it's a highly sensible investment and a protection; but there are those for whom a house is a liability: a ghastly cause of Outgoings from whose roof slates fall off onto litigious persons.

YOU WERE DEAD FOR TWO MINUTES. THE HOUSE IS HERS !
LOAMLEY BUILDING SOCIETY

Long-term, you can't really lose on buying your own house, unless you go for something that's wildly too grand or about to fall off the edge of a cliff. But an earnest young money-minded lady should think twice before hanging a mortgage round the neck of a man who may not be sure he's ready to marry anyway. She might find she's got a house, all right, but no husband; here, as elsewhere, feelings are as important as facts.

Incidentally, if someone asks you actually to *guarantee* a mortgage watch out. You could get stuck with the payments, do you realise, but at the end of it all the house would still be theirs not yours. *Don't do it* without professional advice. A friend of mine underwrote the mortgage of her latest husband's payments on her/their house; he pushed off; she realised she could pay out for twenty years and he'd own it in the end. 'It cost me £15,000 to get out of that marriage,' she bitterly recalls.

LIFE INSURANCE

The second most important thing to know about life insurance is that the people who sell it get the most commission on policies least likely to be the right ones for you. They are highly trained snakes with an answer to your every objection: I'm tempted to say you should kick them off your doormat as if they had yellow fever and slam the phone down if they ring.

Unfortunately the first most important thing to know about life insurance is that unless you are one of the 'childless, single and tax dodgers – three affronts to natural justice', as Alexander Walker said of the footloose, you really do need some; so the above suggestions have to be somewhat modified – unless your lifestyle is so simple that you could cheerfully live on social security if you had to. And *stays* simple, what's more: in old age you may need a lot more in the way of bath-chairs, gin, paid help or taxis than you ever did in your jeans-wearing youth.

If you're on your own, you want something simply for your old age – check whether you have a pension at work. You can consider topping it up with increased contributions. If you're self-employed, or in non-pensionable employment consider a 'Section 226' policy, because its premiums are totally tax-deductable.

If you're a couple, it's more complex. As many a woman knows to her cost, it's hard enough to get your bloke to think about his own death at all, let alone sensibly. With the same sort of superstition that makes elderly women think that if they make a will, they'll die, a young man often feels, deep down, that a policy would in some sinister way bring on his death. So plenty of us say, look, it's not your death, don't you see, it's your old age, to which we are both looking forward, no?

Money differs from an automobile, a mistress or cancer in being equally important to those who have it and those who do not.

J. K. Galbraith

BUT if you get just a savings endowment type of policy, it will actually not pay out nearly enough if the breadwinner does drop off his twig ere the fledglings have left the nest. A lump sum that seems a lot when you take out the policy may be about the equivalent of one year's salary, if you're suddenly left to cope alone; and a fat lot of good *that* is. For more realistic cover at a relatively cheap premium **term insurance** is a better bet – for example a **family income benefit** policy can give the widow an income over a fixed stretch of years – the years, that is, when she'll have to be supporting the children.

The snag is supposed to be that once the fixed term is over, if your husband is still among those present but wheezing around on crutches and the insurance people don't like the look of him, he may not be able to renew it. But there are some which can be bought which *are* renewable and convertible and increasable without further medical examination – more expensive, alas.

If you haven't got any dependants, that doesn't mean you don't want a pension: for example, if your firm's one is lousy or you may be changing jobs – job-changers, sadly, do very badly on company pensions. Should you go for a lump sum or an income? You can't take it *all* as a lump anyway; you might think you could do interesting things with a big bundle of money, but remember that if you invest it, the income counts as *un*earned income, with consequent tax, whereas your pension itself counts as earned.

Remember that the family will be almost equally knocked sideways if *either* of you die – think of having to hire housekeepers etc.; so really you should have two single life policies, one each.

Incidentally, if your employer will not allow you to make additional pension contributions and you do not qualify for a Section 226 policy you might go for a SAYE – Save As You Earn – arrangement, which operates over a five-year period – and preferably National Savings rather than Building Society, because their schemes tend to have a slightly higher gross interest rate than Building Societies. Then if you suddenly decide to hell with your old age, you're going to Tahiti, you can grab the money and run.

See also p. 81 Salting it away and p. 77 Retirement.

Money is better than poverty if only for financial reasons.

Woody Allen

STARTING A FAMILY

The government maternity grant is so low that it's almost a form of contraception in itself – £25; but you may as well claim it – any time after fourteen weeks before the expected date of the birth. The maternity allowance (£25 a week) you may get if you've been working. It's paid for a period of eighteen weeks from the beginning of the eleventh week before the week in which the baby's due. If the baby comes early, it's still the same eighteen weeks, but if it's late, you remain entitled until the end of the sixth week after the birth, but you have to put in an extra claim. It's not taxable.

If a fond grandparent asks what can it give for the baby, try and steer her off bootees and onto a nappy service – even with disposables you need some cloth ones, and you're weak as a kitten to start with. Baby equipment – pram, cot, bath etc. – is usually advertised on the walls of clinics or playgroups and the baby won't know it's second-hand, after all. If you're by any sad chance on Supplementary Benefit, and buying the equipment, even second-hand, would reduce your savings to less than £500, they'll make a payment towards this; unsupported mothers get an extra family allowance for the first child (as well as the additional person's tax allowance, see p. 63) – don't forget to claim it.

Babies don't, actually, cost all that much to begin with; but don't be fooled – they will cost a packet later on. If by any chance you're not feeling broke at this moment, try putting the family allowance into a savings account against the day when every time you take your eye off them they grow out of a pair of shoes.

The older they get, the worse it becomes. But it's if you think you may have to pay for their schooling that the thing gets really drastic. The best way of spreading the agony is probably to start contributing to a school fees insurance policy on your way out of the maternity ward. The trouble is that you don't *feel* rich at that point, especially if the mother has just stopped working; and besides, at that halcyon stage, you assume this particular tot will be so brilliant that it will either be heaped with scholarships, or effortlessly transcend the state system.

If you do decide to insure, you can take out the kind of policy where you pay small amounts each year and it then tots up. The ones for a particular school are usually slightly cheaper than the general ones – but suppose Quentin *didn't get in* to Charterhouse? Or you changed your mind about schools? Best bet is to go for one from a specialist agency – School Fees Insurance Agency, 10 Queen Street, Maidenhead, for example, or Charles Howard and Partners, 177 Regent Street, London W1.

If you've actually got the cash in hand, you can allocate a lump sum so you wind up paying less eventually – they've had the interest on your money meantime. You, by the same token, of course have not – but I'd fight shy of cute schemes designed to 'invest' the schooling money – a lot of parents got stung in the seventies by buying insurance policies linked to the financial market, so when the market slumped, so did their 'savings'. You can get a grandparent to covenant (though I understand they're doing it less these days – I suppose they're all broke too). The Foreign Office or multi-nationals pay the fees for their overseas people. You might take out a second mortgage on your house – many do; but not if you can't trust yourself not to make the kid's life a misery because the very roof over your heads is in pawn to his chances of Achieving.

If you really need private education and you haven't got the money, there are various bursaries and scholarships around: ask the school you're interested in what it might possibly offer. There is an Assisted Places Scheme – get a list from The Truman and Knightley Educational Trust Ltd, 76–78 Notting Hill Gate, London W11 or from the Gabbitas-Thring Educational Trust Ltd, 6 Sackville Street, London W1 (who do a little bursary work of their own, though mainly for topping up other scholarships that aren't quite enough). The Assisted Places Scheme, though, carries a pretty stringent means test and there are only some 230 schools that do it.

If you suddenly hit hard times and can't pay the fees tell the Head: schools are admirably reluctant to heave a child into the street the term before their A-levels; a local authority – particularly ILEA – may pay boarding fees in a family catastrophe if the child really needs boarding, e.g. one parent is in Greenland and the other drunk in a gutter; or in crisis write to the Professional Classes Aid Council, 10 St Christopher's Place, W1 – but *don't* just write and tell them you're hard up, they've heard that too often. The School Fees Insurance Agency is charitable as well as commercial and might have some ideas, and ISIS, 56 Buckingham Gate, London SW1 is, as its name says, the Independent Schools Information Service generally – start your enquiries there.

Even if you reckon you can afford to pay some school fees, it's worth considering two things. First, which *bit* of education do you want it for most? Precious few these days can simply lock several children into the private system at five and cause them to emerge at eighteen. You might send the children to state primary schools, say, then pay for secondary education – either because you wanted, in the words of one forthright teacher, 'to avoid thin and trendy teaching at the stage when they should be solidly *learning*' or to keep a girl, perhaps, out of a tough comprehensive 'where she'd lose her cherry at 13 without knowing what it's all about' (parent speaking). By sixteen the girls may well be getting restive in their sex-free convents, the boys fed up with Play the Ball, and both could perfectly well make it in a comprehensive college, a polytechnic or some other sixth-form college.

A few parents, their sights firmly set on the A-stream of a country comprehensive that doesn't believe in mixed-ability teaching, play it the other way round – they put their kids into the private sector early, to bring them to the top of their form by 11. This works *if* it happens to suit your child – but you'd probably need professional advice to decide whether it did. Cost, by the way, is no guide to quality in prep-school *or* senior – if only because the old and well-endowed may well be cheaper than St Swingalong's, founded 1950.

The second thing is more tenuous. You have a little financial leeway; you want to benefit your child – but *are* school fees always the best way to spend the money? Judith Stone and Felicity Taylor wrote a fascinating article in the *The Observer* some years ago about all the other ways you

STOP
CHILDREN
CROSSING
ADOLESCENT
EMERGENCY
CRIPPLING
INTROSPECTION
HERE'S YOURS NOW!

could spend £1,000 a year (which is what private school fees were then) to your child's benefit. Her suggestions included converting the attic so the child has a TV-free room of its own to work in; extra dance or fencing lessons; an encyclopaedia or an account at a bookshop; foreign trips; a minicab account to shunt child plus cello to music lessons; an emergency fund saved for contact lenses or a nose bob 'to liberate an adolescent from crippling introspection' (fancy; I didn't think you *could*). Even if it was fees in the end, it might be a crammer's – which even Etonians, please note, have been known to need for University entrance.

In any event, it's worth thinking out whether it really makes sense just somehow to scrape together the school fees and have nothing left over for any sort of extras or leisure or fun. You can't, however much you pay, ensure that your child will end up happy, well-adjusted or even educated; you might do better with something in hand to keep your options open.

MONEY FOR THE CHILDREN

What about the money you pay to the children themselves? *Where?* did a survey on pocket money which suggested that the higher up the social ladder people were, the less they gave their children – an equation distorted, I dare say, by the fact that the really affluent may have godparents whose presents coolly wreck the parents' character-forming parsimony.

Some sense can be got into the situation by basing all pocket money on **the value of the Mars bar** – one bar at age five, say; if the bar goes up, that's inflation, and the pocket money goes up too. Or you can give them what seems like a generous sum but insist they put something into a **savings account**. This not only instils Good Habits (you hope) but means that when they want to buy something utterly loony they can learn the hard way how it feels. Also, as soon as possible get them to buy boring things – fares, socks – as well as sweets and records. The conviction that all money is for spending on interesting things is what gets an awful lot of people into the hands of the receiver.

Whatever you've been giving them before, once they're into their teens, they will start clamouring for more; and the distracted parent really doesn't know what's reasonable. You can ask other parents, ones you approve of – there'll always be one blighted kid flashing tenners around in any school; you can – and should – insist that any child wanting more makes out a case for it by keeping accounts for a few weeks. After sixteen, unless they're desperately close to exams, you might think they could go out and do odd jobs for extra money – and there's no harm in letting them earn money from you, provided it's for

---

You can't think rationally on an empty stomach and a whole lot of people can't do it on a full one either.

Lord Reith

things they would not normally do as part of the general work of the house – painting a room, say, cutting the grass or cleaning the car.

When they start wanting expensive clothes is the time to put them on their own allowance – some kids it's twelve, some not till seventeen; but if they want something expensive, whether it's drums or boots or a black leather jacket, it concentrates their minds wonderfully if you offer to pay half (or more) provided they put in some of their own money. Better to say 'OK, but it's expensive – do you want it to be your Christmas present?' than to launch immediately into abrasive rows about why it's a waste of money.

By the way – when they do start proper work, it is not much of a kindness not to claim back part of their pay for their keep. Not much, perhaps – but if they never realise that wages which sound princely while they're living at home will scarcely pay the rent once they move out, they may hit bad trouble later on.

If you are still shelling out when they turn 18, you can **covenant** for the allowance you give. That's to say, if you want the lad to get £100, you pay £70 – the post-tax sum – and he claims back £30 from the revenue. You have to covenant for six years (unlike charities, where the same thing works, but you can do it for three). So what happens if he runs

THIS WASTE OF MONEY OR THAT WASTE OF MONEY?
10% DISCOUNT IF YOUR MUM/DAD AGREE TO PAY HALF OR MORE ON ANY ARTICLE!

away to sea? In theory, he could sue you if you stop paying him. In practice, nothing happens, and the revenue just shrugs its shoulders.

Should someone leave your children a bit of money, you may wish to invest it for them – see p. 81 Non-taxpayers. Don't put any of your money in their names without thinking twice – banks *won't* release their money till they're seven, and while National Savings will, they make an awful fuss about it, insisting on getting the little one's paw-marks on the papers first.

An American used to boast that his son was so bright, he made a dollar every week: 'I give him car fare and he runs behind the streetcar and saves the dollar.' 'I can tell you how he could save ten dollars a week,' said a friend. 'Give him ten dollars for taxi fare and have him run along behind a taxi instead.'

SPORT AND LEISURE

You can spend a fortune on skiing before you've even seen the snow; even jogging seems to demand the right togs to jog in. Every parent knows the blackmail that can be brought to bear by a child deprived of the right running shoes. What, actually, is reasonable?

It helps to realise that there's terrible exploitation by some clothing manufacturers, who go all out for contracts to supply popular football teams and then produce over-priced kits for the kids; this blackmail ought to be resistible. Same with boots: if it's got someone's name on it, you can bet *your* boots it's overpriced. Best train your child for rugger, where rags are practically *de rigeur*. My expert says, though, that it does matter to have the right shoes for the right game, even if they're cheap ones – not just track shoes for everything.

Equipment's trickier, because a keen tennis player really does do better with a good racquet – but if they're poor performers they won't suddenly become centre-court with a new one. Most sports retailers give 10% reduction for certain clubs, but you have to remember to ask for it; sports journals have lots of special offers and sales; and the normal good value cheap places – C & A, Marks and Sparks – have good sportswear. If your kid wants something really fancy, the usual rule applies – say 'OK – if you pay half'.

Local authority Sports and Leisure Centres are a good bet all round – you can often hire equipment, you can try out a sport before you invest a fortune in the gear. Get all the info you need about those and classier clubs from the local authority Leisure Department. But no sport, he adds gloomily, is free. Except one.

What about holidays? It's a vast subject, but a few simple points are

---

I didn't realise that life was a roller-coaster and not a trolley-car.

Richard Benjamin

---

worth making. First, it's almost always cheaper to go on a package than work the thing out bit by bit – but that doesn't mean you've got to go in a glad gang; a package may mean only fare and some lodging. Travel agents aren't as knowledgeable as they seem so it pays to check out several (ask if they are members of ABTA, to make sure they'll still be there when you go back to collect the tickets); for air fares ring the Air Travel Information Bureau, though they don't always know the very cheapest.

Insure your holiday unless you simply don't care if you lose your money (if you or your mother gets ill, for instance); and if you're going abroad insure for medical expenses. Yes, I know they have reciprocal arrangements with some European countries – but they work on a pay-you-back-later basis – and they don't always pay you the lot (the self-employed aren't included in the reciprocal arrangement anyway).

Third, the rule about asking What Am I Really Paying For? applies to holidays doubled in spades. Picturesque self-catering chalet may mean only a change of sinks; if you passionately want the sun don't go to somewhere like Scotland where it only *might* not rain. If one holiday's more expensive than another, is it because it's a better hotel? Because it's August? Because it's to hell and gone, and the air fare's enormous? There was a spot of bother in some remote African country a while back and a hotel-ful of Brits were asked how it affected them. Not at all, it turned out, they were *all* sitting all day by the hotel swimming pool, just exactly as if they'd been in Torremolinos or San Remo. But I bet it cost them a fortune.

You might be tempted by **Time-share** which seems to offer you a cheap holiday home of your own. Not so. Remember that you don't own it in the normal sense: you can't paint it or change it or go there whenever you like – anything but. You're often able to swap with some other time-sharer in a different spot, but who says you want a self-catering holiday of that type for ever? For that's all you're doing – buying, in advance, one particular type of holiday for the foreseeable future. There's never a guarantee that the service charges won't go up – there couldn't be; and as for guaranteed maid service – do they own them as slaves, then?

If you would know what the Lord God thinks of money, you have only to look at those to whom he gives it.

Maurice Baring

TIPPING

Things to hold in mind: (1) the people being tipped aren't embarrassed, it's part of their income (2) *and* they are probably taxed on what it's estimated they get, so you're doing them down if you're too frozen to cough up (3) when in doubt, stick to 12½% (4) it always helps to say 'thank-you' as well.

Right: here goes. **Restaurants**: see if any service is added to the bill; if it's more than 10% that will do, if it's just 10% and they've been nice, add a bit extra – up to 12½%. **Ladies rooms**: what she's put hopefully in the saucer – or less. **Porters**: 50p a piece of luggage. **Taxis**: 10–20p in the pound, unless they've gone round by Land's End or unduly wearied you with how blacks are responsible for inflation. **Hairdressers**: about 12½% divided as: twice as much for stylist as for the girl who gets soap in your eyes (for a shampoo and set); for perms, treatments, etc. the proportion is that the perm girl will get 70% of what the stylist gets, the wash girl 50% – in good establishments they sort it out between themselves anyway. If it agonises you, leave it all at the desk with the words, 'Would you be kind enough to give this to the people? Thank you SO much'. **Sleepers**: 50p second class, £1 first, unless he's woken you one and a half hours before the train gets in so he can get his little cups washed. **Removal men**: about £2 a head. **Coal, delivery men** etc. – don't. **Dustmen, postmen, milkmen** etc. – only at Christmas, £1 up, not much below £3 for the dustmen or they'll spread your garbage all over the garden. **Garages**: nothing for petrol, £1 – £2 for mechanics if especially helpful. **AA men**: in theory nothing, but you could offer two or three pounds if they've laboured for ages in the snow: 'Warm yourself up with this' is the line.

INSURANCE

When the middle classes, feeling poor, wring their hands and wonder what it is the working classes don't spend money on, that seems to leave them with so much more cash in hand, one of the answers is – insurance. Certainly there are few more utterly boring ways to spend money.

But actually you need insurance for you to be carefree – so that you aren't worried sick if the water's coming through the ceiling or your student son's broken his leg in foreign parts. Like having all your plugs changed to safety ones, so that you can let your toddler stuff its pudgy fingers where it likes, insurance is a hedge *against* worry – if it's not so expensive that you worry even more about paying it.

You'd be amazed what you can insure: film stars insure their teeth or legs; you can insure against it raining at the church fête – Pluvius policies they're called (Eagle Star or Lloyds do them) – against getting sloshed and losing your licence (Chauffeurplan Ltd, 17c Curzon Street, London W1 8AQ); you can insure your pet's health (Pet Plan, 35 Horn Lane, London W3 9TA). You can (and should) insure the contents if you have a vast freezer, and things like Hoover Owners Club are effectively a way of insuring against huge repair bills. You are simply betting an insurance company you will lose your mink or fall off the jetty – they're betting that you won't.

They're all worth having and some of them – insuring the contents of your house, and its fabric against fire, motor insurance against third party liability and (if you've any sense) accidental damage to your car – are musts. But it's a minefield. You insure your jewellery, lose a valuable

---

Simply by not owning three medium-sized castles in Tuscany I have saved enough money in the last forty years *in insurance premiums alone* to buy a medium-sized castle in Tuscany.

Punch, 29 May 1974

---

ear-ring and find they'll pay up only half unless you've had the 'sets and pairs' clause deleted specially. (My father once talked an insurance company out of this by asking them if they only paid half if a man burned only one leg of a pair of trousers: 'I suppose he might find a one-legged man but I don't see how that helps my daughter' – but usually you can't.) You insure your domestic contents, start up a tiny knitting business and find, when the wool goes on fire, that the 'business use' has invalidated your whole policy.

A lot of people are under-insured, mainly because they don't bother to think about it; and then they come up against a horrible thing called the principle of average. Suppose you insure your house contents for £5,000 and half of them get nicked. They're insured, as most things are today, as 'new for old' replacement value, so you work out that they will cost £3,500 to replace. Oh no you don't, says the company, you said £5,000 was the total so half of that's only £2,500. Nasty. Make sure the stuff you insure is properly valued – and that it *is* new for old: some old policies may not be.

With household contents and motor insurance it really pays to shop around – the way they rate your job, sex, car etc. may vary so much that there would be £100 difference between two quotes. It's here that, in my own experience, a good insurance broker is a godsend, because they know all this stuff and have keen eyes for the fine print, though *Which?* readers seemed to get on OK without. But even here, beware. Take care with anyone who calls themselves by a fancy title other than broker, i.e. 'Insurance Consultant', say, or 'Associates' (you can check whether he has registered under the Insurance Brokers Registrations Council Act). Why? Because since 1981 anyone calling himself a broker has to keep certain rules, for example keeping your money in a separate account from his own, so that if he goes up the spout your cash doesn't go too. This matters more than you might think, because if the rotten man has gone bust without forwarding your premium, you might not even *be* insured the night the roof falls in.

It seems too simple to mention, but do *claim.* A cigarette burn ruins your carpet – fire insurance. Children throw bricks through your window – house contents. But you mightn't think of it. Claim all you can.

Health insurance

You may think that when you're ill the NHS will take care of everything and you won't cost much money to anyone because (boo-hoo) you'll only be drinking gruel and eating the grapes provided by sympathetic friends. If so, that just shows what a strapping healthy chap you've always been; reality is much nastier. Even an illness that falls somewhat short of the Black Death can be a quick way of joining the deserving poor.

Your job may have a sickness pay scheme, and in any case your employer has to pay out the first eight weeks of sick pay and then claim it back from the state. Then you get Sickness Benefit from your local DHSS and by the time you've been ill for six months, you switch to Invalidity Benefit on the state, and the chances are your firm's scheme is coming to an end. If you've a family, you're going to be in bad trouble: you want an income while you're ill, and **permanent health insurance** can provide it, even if your illness lasts the rest of your working life. Ask whether the policy allows for any index-linking when you take it out (a few do), and make sure it covers your tendency to climb rocks on holiday or drink a pint of whisky a day. If you're self-employed and/or have a young family, this one's a must.

What about accident insurance? Don't – get term life insurance (to pay out on death) and the above-mentioned sickness insurance instead. There are some sick pay policies which offer to pay out if you're in hospital, but by itself that's not much use: they sling you out of hospital pretty sharply these days, but you could still be unfit to work for ages. Still, such insurance is often offered (by the AA, for example) with something else that's far more use: an insurance that pays for private hospital bills if (and only if) the NHS queue for your particular operation in your particular area is too long – six weeks, say. If you're an emergency, you probably do just as well under the Health Service as on the private anyway. Big hospitals have the same intensive care units for all, and if you're really ill you may even be safer in a ward: I know a chap who nearly killed himself because he was stuck away in a remote private room, and when he thrashed his way out of his equipment (owing to lack of alcohol, poor fellow, but we needn't go into that) there was no-one near to shout for a nurse.

By the same token, the young and fit are not so likely to need **medical expenses insurance**, since they're a lot more likely to come off a motor bike or have their noses broken than to suffer from slow, unromantic, painful diseases like arthritic hips or varicose veins, which the Health Service is in no hurry to heal. You may think it's a crying shame that anyone should need BUPA or Private Patients Plan or Western Provident or BCWA (Bristol Contributory Welfare Association) at all, but the hard fact is that since they cracked down on private rooms in NHS hospitals, the private sector has been booming; all the signs are that as time goes on the privately insured will be more and more relieved to be so.

His hands are insured for thousands but he suffers from athletes foot.

US advertisement

The case for getting onto a scheme before you are actually collapsing is that they will *keep* you on their books long past the age at which they would *take* you on. BUPA has 34 subscribers over 100.

I'm inclined to think there ought to be an H. M. Bateman cartoon 'The man who paid the full premiums for BUPA', because there seem to be so many schemes for paying less – group schemes at work, motoring clubs, trade associations, Access, Barclaycard and Trustcard users; check around and see if you can't get 25% reduction at least. An additional advantage is that if you're part of such a group, they may not question you nearly so closely about how much of a wreck you are already.

There is, of course, a limit to all this; however prudent the policies are, you don't want to pay out so much of what you earn that you'll end up thinking it will be a great waste if nothing awful does happen to you. The only two things in life that are certain, said Benjamin Franklin, are death and taxes; hard to do anything (for yourself) about either. And there was a woman (this is true) who had an underground nuclear shelter in America; it had a deep-freeze filled with enough food for months. 'But in the event of a nuclear holocaust,' said a puzzled friend, 'wouldn't there be some doubt about the electricity supply – it might go bad?' 'Oh that's all right,' she said. 'It's all insured.'

I detest life-insurance agents; they always argue that I shall some day die, which is not so.

Stephen Leacock

WHEN THE CRASH COMES

You were in work, or married, you were muddling along all right; and suddenly it all goes wrong. No job, or your man walks out on you, or the breadwinner falls off a ladder and won't work for a year. Perhaps for the first time in your life you're really up against it – not just a laughing reference to the overdraft but a serious possibility of the bailiffs taking your furniture.

When the crash comes, first make sure you've got all the money to which you might be due – if you have been quite well off you may be quite unclued about state benefits, but now's the time you need them. Can you get unemployment benefit? It's paid for up to a year, apply on form B1 from your local Department of Employment Office – actually called Unemployment Benefit Office. Have you got redundancy money? Even if the firm's gone bust you should get what's due to you from the State Redundancy Fund.

There might also be a rent or rate rebate (no, you don't have to be a council tenant) or Family Income Supplement if you've kids, though only if you're working. If a man's not working but his wife is, you can perhaps switch the major tax allowance over to her.

Failing all that, you may well be due for Supplementary Benefit, and you can forget all the nasty things you ever said about state scroungers: you've paid your insurance and your taxes, it's your right. Get form B1 if you are unemployed, or SB1 if it's anything else from a post office or a Social Security office. And there's a host of other possibilities: help with fuel if you've an old or disabled person or a child under 5 or live in an especially unheatable house; your rent or the interest on your mortgage

---

Money doesn't always bring happiness. People with ten million dollars are no happier than people with nine million dollars.

Hobart Brown

BAWPS MILL 1889
BEST BET LUMP SUM INVESTMENTS
GOLDEN HANDSHAKE PLACEMENTS LTD
REDUNDANCY PAYMENTS
USE YOUR
INVESTIT LTD
WHERE TO PUT IT!
TREBLE YOUR CAPITAL
INVESTMENT ADVICE

will be paid direct – it's called Housing Benefit; and Supplementary Benefit is a passport to a whole lot of other things like free prescriptions and free school meals.

If you have redundancy money or savings that are over £3,000, you will be appalled to hear that you can't get Supplementary Benefit; but *don't* rush out and blow it on a car or a holiday – they'd regard that as frivolous and rate you as if you still had it. Better use it to pay debts off or some of the mortgage. If you've a life insurance policy they will, dammit, take its surrender value above £1,500 into account – but (a) that isn't usually much, and (b) you don't actually have to surrender it. What you should do, though, is to *ask* its surrender value without committing yourself; or you could ask to have it converted into a paid-up policy – i.e. if you were half-way through a twenty-year policy, you can ask them to regard it as a fully paid-up ten-year one.

What about your debts? Do you owe the gas board, the HP, the mortgage? There's a golden rule about this which is GET IN FIRST – go and say you're in trouble and what do they suggest? There are various ways the debt can be spread but it all works *only* if they haven't already started to disconnect you or sell the house over your head. (They're not supposed to disconnect heating if you've got an old or disabled person or a small child, or are unemployed or on Supplementary Benefit, without discussing it first; but you can't count on it.)

Having owned up, you then have to work out how to pay it all back. There's a new grim skill called Debt Counselling which sorts out people who've got themselves in a real mess; there aren't enough such counsellors to go round yet, but you can do it for yourself if you're determined. First, work out exactly how much is coming in per week – and make sure you've got all possible benefits. Then you work out, again in weekly terms, exactly what it costs you to live: so much for heat, light, food, fares – everything. The difference between what's coming in and what you must spend each week will be pretty small – but that's what you've got to use to clear yourself of debt.

So you work out the *proportion* of the total debt bill that is owed to each outfit. If you owe £100 to the gas people, £50 each to the electricity and rent, and have £4 a week to spread among them, the gas would get £2, the others £1 each. They'll accept this, because they know it's the only way they'll get anything back – but you have to stick to it, and *don't* be too optimistic about what you can manage. Why bother to do this proportional thing? Because they'll all press you to give them a larger share – you can keep them at bay by showing them it's fair. Commercial

---

It is not a custom with me to keep money to look at.

George Washington

---

companies will press you hardest, because there isn't a lot they can do *except* press you; the loan sharks don't press you at all – why should they? The more in debt you are, the more interest you'll have to pay them, for years and years if not for ever. The electricity people may be able to put in a meter that's set for you to pay more on all the electricity you use till the debt's paid off, but it isn't always technically possible.

The rates, by the way, are the one bill you should *never* leave unpaid, since rates and non-payment of maintenance or tax or court orders are also the only things you can actually go to prison for; and before then they may send the bailiffs round for your furniture. If you've got a bank manager go and talk to him; go and talk to a Citizens Advice Bureau or Consumer centre – and do be honest about the full horror of it all. The agency can negotiate a system of repayments with your creditors on *their* credibility – but if you've not told them about one unpaid bill or the HP on that sofa, the whole thing can come unstuck.

Don't ever think, by the way, that letting firms repossess a thing that you're buying on HP (which they can only do if you've paid less than a third of the payments) is an easy way out – you'll still owe. You had a £1,000 car on HP, so with interest you were set to pay £1,200; let's say you've paid £100. They repossess and sell the car cheaply at auction (good bargains at repossession auctions) for £700. So they've got £700 + £100, *and you still owe them £400.* If it's a credit loan, that's different, thank heavens, because the thing was yours from the start.

SPLITTING UP

Sorting out the money may not be the worst thing about splitting up, but it certainly rubs salt into all the other wounds. If it's conceivably possible for a husband and wife to agree what partition arrangements they want, and then just get them rubber-stamped by the Court, they may avoid not only unnecessary bruising but unnecessary expense as well.

There are several good reasons for keeping the legal intervention down to a minimum. Some people with simple divorces even manage without any. The first is it's expensive; free Law Centres don't do matrimonial work, and you won't necessarily get legal aid – if you're not on Social Security they take a look at you to assess poverty, so even Great-Aunt Jemima's revolting ring may get you rated as too rich. Some solicitors won't take legal aid cases anyway – they don't get enough back from the powers that be, they say; and there's also a hideous time-bomb in the thing: if you're given the house as part of the settlement, and then later sell it, they'll come on you for the amount you owe them for legal aid, even if it was years ago (unless of course your husband was ordered to pay your costs at the time). Do they do that, too, if your pay goes up? No, it's just on capital assets, but that's bad enough. If you are paying a solicitor, ask him 'How do you cost your time?' – it could be £60 an hour or more.

Another reason for keeping the legal involvement down is that, alas, what too often puts the bitterness into what might otherwise have been a reasonably well-tempered divorce is lawyers either saying 'But you could get another £500 out of him' or, on occasion, fixing up everything between themselves on the golf course, when it may not be what *you* wanted – or thought you'd asked for – at all. If you and your separating spouse can work out an agreement, then make four copies of it, give one to each solicitor and say firmly, 'We want that'. Any agreement that involves children has to go before a court, so if you can get the part that concerns the children phrased in the right legal language, it can become part of what's known as the consent order – that's what decides who has them, when they're to be visited, how paid for and so on.

If you can't agree between yourselves, how will the court be likely to divide things? Alas, it's extremely hard to say; because as W. M. Harper points out in *Divorce and Your Money*, you can *either* have absolute predictability – the law always does thus and so – *or* flexibility, but not both; and at the moment the law is trying hard to be flexible and take account of different circumstances. The starting point is still the one-third rule: that's to say, the wife gets one-third of their joint incomes (you aren't going to believe this, but the statement where this is enshrined explains that a man needs more, because he has to hire someone to do his household chores). The home will usually stay with whoever has the children – doesn't make any difference whose name it's in. But it's a toss-up.

Tax

Once you are well and truly separated, a wife with a child (or any other lone mother) can claim an '**additional personal allowance**' on top of her single person's allowance; this brings her up to the level of a man with a married man's allowance. She also gets extra child benefit for the first child. If a wife and/or children are to receive maintenance (I'm saying 'wife' throughout, though it is just occasionally the other way round), there are four ways in which it can be taxed.

With **voluntary maintenance**, the wife doesn't pay any tax, but the husband can't get tax relief on what he pays either. With **small maintenance payments** (it was up to £33 when this book went to press) he claims tax relief, but she has to pay tax on the money if it brings her income into a tax bracket at all. With **large maintenance payments** the husband deducts tax at the basic rate and then the wife can claim that amount back from the Revenue – but it's tiresome, because it takes forever; and she needs a certificate from him before she can claim it, and if he's feeling stroppy he may not supply it. And there's **payment direct to the children**, which is infinitely the best bet because then it counts as their income and towards their tax liability; and unless they are rich little tots they haven't got any such liability. So make sure you get the children's maintenance paid direct to the children, *not* to the wife for the children.

There are further complexities, of course; for example if maintenance is drawn up under a Deed, it counts as 'Large' whatever size it is. And you may have to struggle like a gaffed salmon to make sure that whichever one of you is actually paying the mortgage payments gets the tax relief for them – talk to the tax man, talk to the mortgage company. A wife may need to get her tenancy registered in her name to stop her husband selling the place over her head.

You may think, if you're a separating wife, that you don't want any maintenance for yourself, that you'd far rather be independent; but your solicitor may suggest, all the same, that you claim 50p a year, and there's some sense to it. Because, if circumstances change, you can then go back to the court and get it varied – and suppose you lose your job or fall sick while you're still stuck with the expensive tastes of your joint offspring? It's a useful precaution.

If you simply wake up one morning and find your husband has gone and there isn't a pound in the house, get down to your local Social Security office (in the phone book, under Health) – don't write, it takes too long; they'll give you an appointment and try and sort things out. They do have it in their power to make an Urgent Needs Payment, and normally whatever benefit they reckon you should get starts the Monday following your claim. Take all the bits of paper with you – children's birth certificates, rent book or mortgage documents, family allowance book, the lot. You don't need a legal separation for these realists – just being separated will do. If you're worried sick about debts, see what name is on the bill – if it's your husband's you may not be liable. They may *try* to tell you that you were a 'beneficial user' but I'm told this hasn't actually any basis in law.

In any doubt, write to One Parent Families, 255 Kentish Town Road, London NW5; they seem to know more about it than most solicitors.

SKINFLINTING

All of us do it some of the time and some poor devils have to do it all the time. Bits of it are miserable, but other strategies do give you a fine feeling of having outwitted the snakes who were trying to get too much money out of you.

When you find yourself poorer than you used to be, the hardest thing is to sort out what parts of your lifestyle could be altered, and which couldn't; it takes a major shake-up to alter habits that you hardly knew you'd got. Advisers who painstakingly try to sort out those who are badly in debt say these people go on blindly doing things which make no sense at all: they buy kitchen paper at 70p a roll (instead of using a rag or loo paper) when they've hardly enough for food; they run the tumble dryer daily because they must wash the boy's only trousers – without calculating that at 16p an hour, they could for the same money buy a secondhand extra pair. They go on assuming that cleanliness is next to godliness, in financial circumstances in which it is next to impossible; and never dream of switching off the immersion heater.

At a slightly different level, there are those who can't imagine living without a car – yet there are such things as mopeds, not to mention bicycles. The telephone – you can get a lock on it, so that lovers or prospective employers can ring in but you (if you've hidden the key) won't be tempted to ring out. What about daily papers? Someone said that getting the news by reading daily papers was like telling the time by the second hand. You need a TV, sure, but it doesn't have to be a big colour one, rather than a small black-and-white. And so on.

For most people, the biggest drain is gas and electricity bills (both Boards get out pamphlets about how to spread the cost). But how can

---

Money speaks sense in a language all nations understand.

Aphra Benn

you just resolve to be cold? You can't – only you can go round screwing up windows you don't need to open or dribbling paint into the draughty cracks; you can put rag sausages along doors, and insulate the loft unless you're actually living in it. If you have to move, so you're buying new curtains anyway, get ones with aluminium linings so the heat's reflected back into the room (you can put aluminium foil on the wall behind radiators with the same effect).

Switch on the immersion only when you need to do a wash, and wash up in a kettleful of water – a habit my mother-in-law has kept since the war; and if you want one cup of tea, why waste ten minutes boiling up the entire kettle? Lag the tank wherever you can (if you're on Supplementary Benefit you can get a grant for this). The double-glazing salesman's claim of saving 50% of heating bills is absurd, but you can put up Acrylic sheeting; or even Clingfilm in the worst of the weather.

All these things may sound a bore, and they are; but there are more interesting ways of spending £5 a week than heating up the air just outside your home.

Apart from becoming a vegetarian, the best way of saving on what you eat is by outwitting your natural tendency to spend like a drunken sailor when you go food shopping. Go with a list, taking only what you plan to spend – no extra, no cheque book. Shop after meals, because people buy far more on impulse when they're hungry; watch for good times of day – Sainsbury's sell off all sorts of salads, for example, around five o'clock

on a Saturday. Supermarkets are cheaper for groceries but not for fruit and veg – but I mean proper supermarkets like Tesco's or Waitrose; Marks and Spencer's has quite an up-market food policy, and those self-service corner shops that stay open all evening are the most expensive of the lot.

One tip: if you cut out something precious to you to save money, keep the money you save separate. Did you ever meet anyone who gave up smoking to save six pounds a week who *had* the six pounds? No, nor did I – but if one puts the pound each morning into what they used to call a Tisbit Box, then it would be at least marginally easier not to spend on the swings what you've just saved by staying off the roundabouts.

All this is cheerless stuff. More fun is bargains – getting clothes from the Oxfam shop or jumble sales; inspired DIY, meaning that with the aid of a handy stapling gun you can cover a set of chair-seats for the price a shop would have charged to do just one; or buying useful furniture in junk shops or sale-rooms or from ads in the local paper (my favourites are office furniture shops: 'Have you got another swivel chair for £1.50?' I asked the man. 'I have,' he said gloomily 'I've got 97, actually'). Get Barty Phillips' *The Bargain Book* (Pan £1.95) which tells you how not to pay the full price for practically anything. And you might also learn to haggle or at least ask for a discount for cash: Barty's brother always does, and it's apparently like that man who went around asking every woman he met to sleep with him: he gets a lot of refusals but an amazing number say yes. The lower end of the British market is now often in the hands of Asians, for whom bargaining seems perfectly natural; you might ask yourself if you can still afford to be quite as British and embarrassed as you have been.

You can cut down; you can live sensibly; but it helps, in the end, to take relentless consumerism with a pinch of salt. Sometimes I read about all these people showering under their hair-rinsers, drawing the curtains as soon as it's dark and bumping around because they're saving the light; driving at exactly 55.5 miles an hour or crawling about at floor level in the supermarkets because they put at eye level the things on which they rake in the most commission, and they scarcely sound like human beings at all. You're not actually under a moral obligation *always* to choose the Best Value if you don't happen to like it.

Do not, however, place too much reliance on Tracy's Law of Diminishing Cost. This Law, propounded by Honor Tracy, describes how you see something you like in a shop window and go in to buy it. You come to your senses in time, however, and get out without spending the £20 it cost. In the next shop you see an even more desirable object that costs £25; you go in; this time you give way and buy it. As you have just saved £20 by not buying the object in the other shop, however, you have got a vastly superior article for only £5.

It is no good going to bed to save the light if the result is twins.

Chinese Proverb

IT'S CHEAPER TO . . . or is it?

Buy things in the sales

Yes, if you actually want them, and would have had to buy them anyway. It's *not* cheaper to get something reduced from £60 to £30 that you'd normally have paid £25 for – better value maybe, but not cheaper. And it especially isn't cheaper to buy four tea towels at 75p instead of £1 and then take a taxi home because you're worn out.

Suspect phrase: 'We could always do with . . .'

Get money from a Servicetill or Checkpoint

Charges across the counter are nearly double what they are from the magic machine outside the banks; but, if you're like me, your finger flicks far too easily to a higher figure . . . and if you're account's over a certain amount in credit, you shouldn't pay anything for a cheque anyway.

Suspect phrase: 'Just to be on the safe side . . .'

Buy in bulk

Yes, sometimes. But you may use far more of something if you've always got stacks of it; and you have to store it somewhere (in plastic sacks? then bang goes your saving). Also, check that it really *is* cheaper – the big size is often not cheaper per oz than the smaller. The pee-bottles of the astronauts had to fit, obviously, but no-one could be shot into space feeling inadequate; so the sizes were called Large, Enormous and Gigantic. Some detergent firms work much the same way.

Suspect phrase: 'So over two years that should save us . . .'

Always watch the unit price, though, can also be questionable advice. This packet of biscuits works out at 10p an oz, that one at 12p – but if the one at 12p an oz contains fewer or smaller biscuits, and the kids will go on eating until there aren't any more, then you're quite right to plump for the cheaper packet.

Suspect phrase: 'It actually works out cheaper per ounce . . .'

Stick to fresh veg and avoid convenience food

It ain't necessarily so. English roots are cheap in midwinter when nothing else is, certainly. But an Olde English Cauliflower could be costing twice as much as frozen florets, fresh tomatoes almost never come down to what they cost in a tin. Hard-up people eat tinned processed peas because they really are cheaper.

Suspect phrase: 'I wouldn't touch that convenience junk . . .'

RAISING THE WIND

You need more money and you need it now. How can you get some?

A loan

Always try the bank first, and if that manager says no try another bank; the first man may have been an anal-retentive stick-in-the-mud, the second not. Get a **second mortgage** – from the same company as does your house, if it's for home improvement; from another company if not. *Don't* go to a loan shark. If you borrow from a **friend or a relative**, put it in writing; as a friend of mine charmingly said as he wrote a receipt: 'The way I drive, I'd like you to have a claim against my estate.' An agreed interest rate saves feeling too beholden.

Sell something

If it's something like a **lawnmower** or a **motorbike**, put up notices in your office (free), a newsagent's (cheap), local paper (not bad), Exchange and Mart (OK). If it's **pictures or antique china**, you'll think about a saleroom – you can take them to Sotheby's or Christie's to be sneered at if you live near London, or find a local saleroom in the Yellow Pages. **Furniture** also goes through salerooms, but when we sold furniture that went for £242, the cheque we finally got, after they'd taken their cut, and the removal man, and VAT and things, was for precisely £8 – sell to a local shop if you can. If there's an **open market** near you, try that – check with whoever runs it, you don't want the local heavies overturning your trestle table. A **garage sale** – not necessarily in a garage – is where you lay out your own jumble sale and invite the public to buy things – or scan the local paper for someone else's and ask if you can join in.

Jewellery is a good thing to sell, but you must be prepared to go from shop to shop and ignore the way they tell you your rubies are worth 75p.

Pawnbrokers exist, and will lend – but only piddling amounts, only on jewellery and gold at that – and only so much per day: go early. If you go over your six months, and they sell the thing, *you* have a right to the money they sold it for, less their charges – they don't tell you that, so you have to go and claim it.

Use your premises

For example, for **babyminding** (a very good one if you're on Supplementary Benefit, as they 'ignore' a large part of earnings made this way). **Granny sitting** is a coming field; you could **rent out a room** (ask for rent in advance) or ask the local social services if they've any **teenagers** they want fostered – it's a hard way to earn the money, but it can be done.

Start up a business

Not by buying an expensive machine but with something you're good at anyway – advertise locally if you make brilliant cakes, or are a dressmaker; a couple near us started selling lunch sandwiches from a big country basket to local firms, another cooks for dinner parties. You could run a gardening service or set up as a china-mender. The black economy sounds bad, but you, too, could become part of what we'll call the informal economy. There's a Small Firms Service run by the Department of Industry – look in the telephone directory or dial 100 and ask for Freefone 2444 for masses of information.

I have to warn you there are dangers and snags in all this: e.g. 'business use' may invalidate your insurance, or your right as an owner-occupier to sell your home without Capital Gains Tax. Go carefully.

Money in a hurry . . .

You can telegraph money orders through a Post Office; abroad, it has to be done through banks, and it costs a lot – and how long it takes depends on the bank in the country you're sending it to. Italy and USA are notoriously bad, though one manager told me he'd got money to a client in ninety minutes once, when the man's son was waiting in a coma in an ambulance outside a Los Angeles hospital which wouldn't take him in till it had the cash (yet another reason for holiday medical insurance). You can get cash on your American Express card at their offices; from banks on your Access or Visa. Marks and Spencer's will cash you a cheque outside bank hours; and banks at airports are also open longer than normal. Change Weschel will cash your cheques, but charge a high percentage.

DESPERATE MEASURES

(The first four of these have actually been tried, and worked – that time, anyway.)

An unexpected bill that you can't pay arrives through the letter box. If you can pay it in a few weeks' time, do what a cellist friend of mine did: he sent the cheque for the mortgage on his cello to the rates people, and vice versa. Each was assured that there *was* a cheque – and it took them about three weeks to sort it all out.

You keep getting this **computerised bill** that you think is wrong. Nothing you say in covering letters has the slightest effect; it remorselessly sends out further demands. What you must do is *staple* your letter to the card, preferably over the number. Then an actual human being has to unstaple it – which is how I finally persuaded the National Car Company I didn't owe it $16. I recently heard of a financial wizard who addressed a computer he was quarrelling with in Chinese, since when he hasn't heard a word; he was rather hoping he might be called in as an expert and paid to do the translation.

Rotate the credit cards. The accountant of a multi-national swears he actually did this – you pay your American Express with your Access, your Visa with your American Express – if only there were twelve, he thought, you'd never need to pay at all. I'm sceptical – but you can certainly do it with those where you can get cash – Visa, Access, American Express.

You can also get a **cheap loan** in much the same way: you get £400 on your Visa; shortly before payment day get £400 cash from Access, add the per cent charge shown on the Visa statement, and pay it. About a week later get £400 from Visa again, and pay Access, adding their per cent – borrow from Visa for seven weeks, Access for a week – it can go on forever. It works out at 12½% roughly.

The cheque is in the post

There are countless ways of sending a reassuring cheque that won't actually be cashed: make the written sum and the number disagree – i.e. £56.40 written as fifty-six pounds fourteen, or post-date the cheque by-accident-on-purpose to the next year – they'll send it back (though it's rash to try this on anyone who might disconnect you). Or post the cheque without the remittance advice, and then, when they protest, send the remittance advice without the cheque. If the prestige address is Toffeenose House, Pall Mall, please pay to P.O. Box 54 Scragsville, send the cheque to the classy address. If all else fails, send them a token fiver and query the bill. They will think that the fiver proves you are only trying to be honest, really . . . it's no wonder they get so cynical in Accounts.

Aubrey Menen, the writer, was educated in England. When he was about twelve his English mother and his Indian father split up, and he was offered a choice: return to England with his mother, or remain in India, becoming the heir to his father's vast estates. To do this, he would have to become a Hindu, undergoing a number of purification ceremonies, including drinking a pint of cow's urine. He chose to go to England. His father asked him why. In particular, he was interested to know whether not wanting to drink the urine had anything to do with it. The boy admitted that it had.

'My boy,' said his father sadly, 'if in the course of your life that's the worst thing you ever have to do for money, you'll be lucky.'

THREE UNHELPFUL ATTITUDES

Tharn

The condition of some rabbits in *Watership Down*, who when in danger became so paralysed with fear that they couldn't leap off in any useful direction. People get that way when faced with bills they can't pay – they put them at the back of a drawer, they refuse to open the envelopes. The Revenue were once reduced to writing to a friend of mine on scented mauve notepaper to tell him of a rebate he could claim, and banks, in despair, post letters on Friday to arrive Saturday, in the hope that a child may pick it off the mat and say, 'What's this letter for Daddy?' What you need in this situation is another rabbit; someone else (probably not your mate) to open the envelopes for you. It probably isn't as bad as you think, and even if it is, it'll get worse the longer you leave it.

The Ziegfield feeling

'Come down to Florida,' wrote a friend of Flo Ziegfield, showbiz magnate, 'Flo's feeling rich'. 'Flo always is,' was the reply. 'The trouble is, it's just a feeling.' This is a particular curse of the self-employed – to feel rich or poor according to how the work's going, not what's actually in the bank. A barrister's wife bitterly attributes their continuing crises to the fact that they spend every fee twice – once when he gets the case, and again when he gets paid. That's no way to deal with cheques – you have to count them in and count them out, as the man on the channel steamer said of his sandwiches.

Pennies in heaven

A girl who was at college with me was asked what kind of engagement ring she'd like: 'Sapphire,' she said. He gave her a diamond one – 'I'm advised that sapphires don't keep their value'. There's a type of well-heeled person who talks as if they were morally obliged to do the most financially advantageous thing – they are 'forced' to leave the country for tax reasons, or sell something pretty because they fear its value will depreciate. It's nonsense. You don't *have* to move money around in various tweak schemes to maximise it, if you'd rather bung it in a building society and get on with something else; you don't *have* to buy the antique French walnut which you find hideous but a good investment, rather than the beautiful modern glass that you will probably break: you just choose to, which is not the same thing. Maybe it was overstating it to say that money is the root of all evil, but the way some people talk as if being prudent was the same as being *good*. . . . If they were really all that good, they'd give it to the poor.

Many have been ruined by buying good pennyworths.

Benjamin Franklin

RETIREMENT

Watching a chap who was rich enough to fly back from Florida for a London party carefully waving his OAP card at the Heathrow tube makes one sometimes wonder if being retired isn't the most advantageous state to be in. Certainly there are quite a few perks – you can get into cinemas cheaper, you can get a telephone rental that's 3p cheaper off any call under a certain number, there's an OAP railcard for cheap fares, there are things like museums and courses where you rate the same as if you were a student.

For all that, it's likely your income goes plummeting down – even if you retire early and get a bit of extra pension under the Job Release scheme (get the leaflets from a Job Centre). When you get to sixty-five (man) or sixty (woman) you'll get the National Retirement Pension on your NI contributions; you'll have any company pension or private insurance pension you'll have laid on for yourself, plus the interest on any money you have squirrelled away; and it will all be put together and taxed. A wife who has paid her own NI contributions gets her own pension, and gets a wife's earnings allowance as before; but if what she gets is on the strength of her husband's contributions, then it's all added to *his* total for tax purposes. If she's not paid enough contributions for a full pension for herself, but has paid some, she'll get more than the wife's pension, in proportion as she's paid. Between 1961 and 1975 they were having a stab at a graduated pension scheme, so if you were paying contributions then you may get that paid with your retirement pension. A woman who is only getting her pension because of her husband's contributions won't get it when she's sixty unless he is by then sixty-five.

You can be young without money, but you can't be old without it.

Tennessee Williams

If you're over sixty-five and your income isn't more than £7,600 (in the current tax year) you get an Age Allowance – higher than the single or married man's – but you have to claim for it. There may be other allowances, too – an extra allowance for a widow on her husband's death or if you're ill or old or have someone living in to look after you. They're insultingly small, but you might as well have them. If you're getting a company pension, all the tax you have to pay will be taken off that, just as it was with PAYE when you were earning.

What if your company offers you part of your pension as a lump sum? Depends if your pension is in any way index-linked. If it is, you're better off with that; but if not, your pension will decline in real value, so if you get your hands on the lump, you can invest it to keep pace. You hope. The only snag is that the investment interest counts as *un*earned income, while the pension itself is earned; so it does rather depend what tax bracket you are in.

If you **go on earning** for a bit, your employer's pension won't be affected but the State pension will – it goes down if you earn more than £57 until you're 70 (man) or 65 (woman). After that they're apparently so astonished you can get anyone to pay you anything that they let it go.

The amount they sting you for investment income goes on just as if you were a strapping thirty year old, including the investment income surcharge, if it applies; there are pamphlets IR4 and IR4A to tell you what the sums are.

If you live in a house that's now a bit big for you when the grandchildren are mercifully not visiting, as a lot of retired people do, you might think of raising a bit of money by letting off a room. You needn't worry about having such cuckoos in your nest forever – you always *can* get a tenant out of a room in your own house, though it may take a bit of time and/or a court order. What you might do, though, if you live in a town where housing's short or anywhere near Higher or Further Education, is consider whether you wouldn't rather have a bit of help, especially as you get older. A student living in a room could do a bit of cleaning, help with the ironing, bring you meals when you're ill and no money need change hands at all. You might take a look at the geography of your home with this in mind, and pay now (while you've still got a bit from your earning years) to put in a fixed basin, say, or a separate entry – you don't necessarily want some ghastly student's hair-dye cluttering up your bathroom, or feel like leaving your door unlocked if she's not planning to be home till 2 a.m. If it's too elaborate,

---

Of great Riches, there is no real use, except it be in distribution; the rest is but Conceit.

Francis Bacon

---

of course, it *could* put your rates up – if it's major, you'd better check with your local Rates Valuation panel. See what your builder says.

If you've no one to leave your home to, or don't much care whether they benefit or not (your children being either rich, revolting or Black Sheep), you might – since you can't take it with you – think about a Life Insurance Home Income Plan (Age Concern have a pamphlet on this, too) – you pledge your house, and get some money to spend and/or an income. This can be tricky, though, so for this you do need expert advice. Alternatively, if you're worried about what happens when you're too frail to cope with it all, there are various schemes for making over your house so that you live in a bit of it, the rest becomes an old folks home and you can stop worrying about who's going to mend the roof. Age Concern will advise.

There's perhaps one more thing that needs saying. The elderly have more experience and more patience than their juniors, but for the best of reasons they may have two strokes against them. The first, obviously, is ignorance of the current scene – it changes so fast, and rules which worked a treat ten years ago may not apply now. It's worth their while to get the two little bibles put out by Age Concern – *Your Rights* (price 70p) and *Your Taxes and Savings in Retirement* (£1.00) – you can get them across the counter at some bookshops or write to Bernard Sunley House, Pitcairn Road, Mitcham, Surrey. You can also go and pester your local PAYE office and/or the DHSS – there is no reason at all to be fobbed off if you don't understand your situation.

The other is pride. A lot of old people hate to take state benefits because they seem like charity – but they're not. They are like insurance payments, something you've paid for and worked for, ones that are yours by right. You wouldn't think it was somehow indecent to claim on a motor accident policy, would you? Well then.

If you can't make ends meet, you're entitled to Supplementary Pension (like Supplementary Benefit, only for OAPs). You might be eligible for a rent and rate rebate – though you don't get that if you're on Supplementary Pension, you get what's called Unified Housing Benefit instead. It's worth working out which way of claiming would benefit you most, and there are quite a lot of other possible benefits connected with heating and so on. Don't forget, either, that age sometimes brings disability – there are important benefits like Attendance Allowance (which isn't taxed) when someone needs a lot of looking after e.g. after a stroke.

They reckon that a *million* pensioners are under-claiming on something that's due to them; it really hurts to think of the Government getting away with all that money.

INVESTMENT

You have got, to your surprise, a lump of money – a big one, a little one; you want to tuck it away till your old age, or just till the ghastly bills come in next January. What should you do with it?

It isn't, alas, something with two or three loud clear answers. *Money Mail Savers Guide*, which is not only informative but actually readable, lists over sixty things you could do with your money, and we can't go into the entire lot here and now. A few pointers might help, all the same. (I'm supposing for the moment that you are a tax-payer – we'll come back later to what you should do if you're not.)

If you want the money in a few months time

If interest rates are high (which they're not, at the time I'm writing this) your bank Deposit Account is OK. A building society Share Account is good value; you get £100–£300 cash on demand and any amount by cheque. There is also a clever thing you can do with Government stock, especially if you're a higher-rate tax-payer; listen carefully to Grandmamma. Government stock pays its dividends twice a year. You get your bank or broker to buy it just *after* the dividend's been paid, when it's therefore cheap. It then increases in value as it comes near to the next pay-out – and you sell it just *before* that. What, no interest? No, but a gain – and up to £5,300 of that is tax free. I'm told if you do it all the time the revenue barks at you, but now and again is OK.

If you are pretty sure you won't want the money for a year or more

Deposit account might still be all right; but you don't know what interest rates are going to do and they're bad value if interest rates are low, even

---

Never invest your money in anything that eats or needs repairing.

Billy Rose

---

if it's in a fancy scheme like Notice Account or Savings Account. Unless you're prepared to keep an eye on it, and move in to something else if interest rates fall, you'd do better in a **building society extra share account**. What happens is that you invest the money for a term of one to six years, BUT you can get at it at three months' notice (with some loss of interest) at any time. For the shorter-term get-out shares, you must usually invest at least £2,000. These are called things like High Return Access Shares, High Option Bonds and so on – read the Building Society's brochures. You could also buy Fixed Interest Government Stock (don't take anything that matures in over ten years or without a fixed date) and these you can sell on the stock market at any time; trouble is, what you get for them in the market depends on what interest rates are doing generally, and there's no way you can know this ahead of time. Local authority loans are sometimes good value, but these, too, you can't cash in ahead of time, only sell them to someone else – and again, the price you'll get depends on interest rates.

Salting it away for the far future

If you've a large sum and you want to put it by, that's probably where you need good professional advice; though never forget that after the early seventies crash the Building Societies ran an ad which said, 'Susan Brown doesn't know much about money, but she's done a lot better this year than a lot of people who do.' You aren't going to *risk* your money if you invest it in Government Stocks, or in granny bonds, or a building society. It would be reasonable to chance some of it in a Unit Trust, which is a scheme to spread the money to a lot of investors among a lot of different stocks and shares, so that you don't risk going down on any one. But if there's a complete market collapse, of course, the unit trusts aren't exempt; *everything* will go down. There's a theory that if you buy some and sell some from time to time you'll be OK, because you'll be buying cheap as well as selling cheap; but I can't vouch for it.

You might consider buying yourself a pension, a **retirement annuity**, if you're not in a company pension scheme, provided you're sure you don't want to touch the money till you're sixty; but remember we live in chancy times – you might want your money sooner if you get made redundant, change mates or wish to sail solo round the world. In any event, you'd have a tussle with your insurance broker, because *they* prefer regular premiums – they get more commission on that.

If you don't pay any tax but have a few shekels to look after, steer clear of Building Societies, since they deduct tax before they pay out and you can't claim it back. Local authority loans, which are often quite good value, also deduct tax but you can claim it back if you've the energy.

Better are things that give you straight interest – bank Deposit Accounts, National Savings Bank Investment Accounts which might not yield much for high taxpayers but are fine for you. Your non-taxed status doesn't give you any advantage with granny bonds – they are just for peace of mind; you also get a lot of peace of mind with short-dated Government stocks – you know you'll be able to get your money back within a given time whatever happens. Finance Companies are a good bet – you can choose between several accounts according to how quickly you might or might not need the money. Finance houses have names like Forward Trust, United Dominions Trust, Lombard North Central. *Not* to be confused with Unit Trusts, who are investing in stocks that may go up and down; these stiff-lipped people stick to the utterly safe.

Who *is* a non-tax-payer? Those with very low incomes; and children, of course, if they aren't earning and haven't more than about £1,500 in income – whatever is the basic single allowance for the year.

Tax-payers or not, rich or skint, keep to these rules:

Whatever you do, don't put all your eggs in one basket.

Whatever you do, don't tie up all your money for too long – you never know what crisis – or impulse – might hit you.

Whatever you've done, keep an eye on it.

From stale of sock . . .

That's how my son used to describe the *From Sale of Stock you get £100* Chance card in Monopoly; in real life, also, too many glittering prospects turn out to have feet of cheese. I can tell you how to buy stocks and shares – you get the bank to do it for you, or write to Public Relations, The Stock Exchange, London EC2N 1HP and they'll give you the names of three firms that take small accounts. But – what are you actually buying?

Security? No; that which goes up may always come down. A chance to be rich? Yes – in much the same way as betting on the horses. It's *enormous* fun playing the market – but it's a game, as even J. M. Keynes (who did it every morning for half an hour in bed, thus doubling the reserves of King's College, Cambridge) admitted.

For the market is not about which firms are going to prosper and which are not. It's about which firms other people will *think* are going to prosper – and will therefore be prepared to pay more for tomorrow than they do today. It is nervous, emotional, subject to strange vibrations. Those who do nothing else with their waking lives except calculate, and watch this market, and guess which way it will jump don't by any means always get it right; how much less you, doing it in your spare time?

If you want to have some fun, fine – but don't commit all your savings to it.

WHO SAYS THEY'RE NOT MAKING LAND ANYMORE!
ESTATE AGENT

Buying baubles

What about other hedges against inflation or hard times – diamonds? Kruggerands? Property? Impressionists? You can forget about Impressionists for a start, because they're far too expensive to buy, let alone insure – and who wants a picture mouldering in a bank vault? Kruggerands, which are just a handy form of gold, became highly over-priced as soon as word got around that they were a fool-proof investment – by the time the news has reached you and me, alas, such things almost always *are* over-priced and nowadays you pay VAT on them, which makes them a much less good bet. Diamonds? No good – *Which?* bought some, and waited, and sold them – in real terms not at a profit. Property? 'Buy land,' said Mark Twain, 'They're not making it any more.' In the long run, I suppose, you can't utterly lose on property, but it depends how long the run. When we were newly-weds we went to look at a flat in a new block whose rent was light years out of our reach; we trudged out feeling very down-at-heel and young and poor. The man who put the block up went on from strength to strength, but a couple of years ago I met him: he was driving me home in a minicab. There's a message in there somewhere.

In general terms, there obviously are things on which you can spend your money that are easier to sell again than others – who wants to buy a second-hand dog? Modern furniture is worth practically nothing a month after you buy it, antiques will always keep some value; an old goatskin rug is quite soon a bit of old (not to say filthy) goat, but a Golden Afghan is a recognisable commodity. Jewels, old silver – they'll always bring in something, though not necessarily what you want when you want it. The question of Liquidity, which means that you do have some reserves you can actually lay your hands on quickly in the form of cash, demands that you never put your all into things like this; the question of being a human being, and not a ruddy calculating machine, suggests you ought to buy things that you will, whatever happens, enjoy possessing.

You could do worse than follow the Anton Felton Law of Purchase which says that anything you buy should be beautiful, and useful, and likely to keep its value. And preferably – since he's a pessimist, i.e. an accountant – portable.

Any girl who was a lady would not even think of having such a good time that she did not remember to hang on to her jewelry . . . kissing your hand may make you feel very good but a diamond and sapphire bracelet lasts forever.

Anita Loos

MORE INFORMATION

As you've gathered by now, this book provides headlines only; but the fine print can be very important. Also, things in the money world *change* – often quite dramatically. A shift in the tax structure, the cancellation of a benefit, or a new gimmick by the mortgage companies can radically change what's a good bet and what's a bad one, so it pays to keep abreast of what's going on. For those who want to read more here are a few suggestions.

Money Which? is a part of the general *Which?* service, and you can become a subscriber for £19 a year; write to the Consumers Association 14 Buckingham Street, London WC1. Also, they now get out *The Which Book of Money*, which is as clear as such a subject can be, and has all the answers; (trouble is, by the time you've been through the detail you're apt to have forgotten the question). It costs £9.95, also from the Consumers Association.

Observer Money is a mine of clear information, £1.20 per issue, £12.50 a year's subscription from Computer Posting Ltd., 374 Wandsworth Road, London SW8 4TE. *Money Mail*, every Wednesday in the *Daily Mail*, has masses for the ordinary puzzled person as well as the city man, and they also get out the *Money Mail Savers Guide*, excellently clear at 90p from Harmsworth Publications Ltd, Carmelite House, London EC4Y 0JA.

The **tax** people get out sheafs of leaflets and these days they are in language that one can understand; worth a visit to your local tax office or a Citizens Advice Bureau to pick up the ones that apply to you.

Similarly, the DHSS get out a pamphlet called *Which Benefit* (nothing to do with the Consumers Association) subtitled '60 ways to get cash help'. Get it from a local social security office or the DHSS Leaflets Unit, P.O. Box 21, Stanmore, Middlesex MA7 1AY. For more detail, there are two comprehensive handbooks from Child Poverty Action group, 1 Macklin Street, London WC2 5NH – *National Welfare Benefits Handbook* and *Rights Guide to Non-Means-Tested Social Security Benefits*; £2.50 each. They'll also answer queries – tel. 01–242 3225/9149. If you have a problem with improvement grants, landlords or whatever, The London Housing Aid Centre (01–373 7276) will tell you which of 120 Housing Aid Centres is nearest to you.

If you have special problems, the chances are there is a special organisation to help you. **Widows** should write to the National Association of Widows, c/o Stafford District Voluntary Service Centre, Chell Road, Stafford, or get hold of the *Handbook for Widows*, which Virago publish for them – it's by June Hemer and Ann Stanyer and costs £1.50.

If you're **disabled**, or have someone disabled to look after, there are quite a few possible benefits – get leaflets from the local DHSS (listed under Health in the phone book) or for information or enlightenment write to the Disability Alliance, 21 Star Street W2 1QB. They're a small, overworked outfit, though, so if you can manage on pamphlets and perhaps a Citizens Advice Bureau, do.

National Council for One Parent Families, 255 Kentish Town Road, London NW5 know all there is to know about **single parents** and **divorced and separated people**; there is also National Council for the Divorced and Separated, 13 High Street, Little Shelford, Cambridge CB2 5ES.

And if you're on your own and coping with an **aged parent**, you need the National Council for the Single Woman and Her Dependants, 29 Chilworth Mews, London W2, who can offer you a lot more than sympathy.

WINDFALLS

Perhaps the most agreeable windfalls are those that aren't big enough to ruin your life, as the lives of football pools winners are reputedly ruined; but give you a chance to fulfil at least one lifelong dream. Here are few ways in which people I know have spent little legacies or small gains.

A middle-aged friend recently came into some money; she had just moved house and the money could well have been absorbed by the new flat. Instead she bought a suede trouser suit, silk shirts, silk underclothes, a fur-lined mackintosh. Folly? Perhaps; but she's upgraded her wardrobe for the next ten years.

A refugee from Hitler suddenly got, umpteen years later, some money from one of those funds with which they recompense Nazi victims. Among other things, she sent a cheque for £100 out of the blue to a couple who had helped her husband leave Austria – and they delightedly spent it on new curtains and bedcovers.

A rather hard-up elderly lady suddenly came into £1,000 – she blew the lot on visiting her daughter in Canada. A don, not starving but with never, ever a penny to spare – he had five children – came into £2,000 and could well have used it all to ease his usual dearth, into which ever-open maw it would have disappeared in about a month. Instead he bought a ramshackle farmhouse in the Dordogne, and he and his family have been restoring it, brick by loving brick, ever since.

The wife of a best-selling thriller writer inherited £2,000 also; as they were fairly well off she didn't need to rush out and buy a car or whatever; she used it to get her teeth fixed by a man she judged to be absolutely the top man in Britain. Now there's so much hidden gold in her smile that she practically has to have Treasury permission to leave the country.

I know a retiring headmistress who put the whole of her lump sum retirement gratuity into the bursary fund of the school – it was going independent and wanted to go on having girls from poor families as well as rich. And I know a man who used a big chunk of his early-retirement money to buy a boat. His family are furious, of course – what about their Old Age? But he reasons that there isn't any other moment, ever, that he would be able to have a boat; which is maybe worth a few electric blankets and bottles of cough mixture when he's seventy.

Tailpiece

Writing this book has had a powerful effect on me. I have become aware of the heat leaking out of the house because of the cracks under the doors; the money leaking out of my life because of the cracks in my thinking. I have suddenly started to worry about whether my pension is big enough and whether we've paid the insurance, where once I would only worry about getting by till my next paycheck. I think I've discovered some ways in which it's senseless to waste money, and I now believe that I Could Try Harder to keep track of what happens to the stuff.

But I am even more certain than I used to be of two basic precepts. The first is Dr Johnson's, of course: that no-one but a blockhead ever wrote but for money. The second is the Chinese proverb that says: 'If you have two loaves, sell one and buy a lily'.

I'd like to live like a poor man with lots of money.

Picasso

INDEX

morale, buying to boost, 8
morals and money, 18